The GIRL *in the* WHEELCHAIR

(It's Not That Bad)

Gillian Mauro

ISBN 978-1-7772836-0-5

CHAPTER ONE

Sixty Seconds Before

MARCH 18, 2010

It was just an ordinary day—nothing fancy, nothing special, nothing overly alarming. I woke up as usual, without a care in the world, having enjoyed the extra couple hours of sleep. I had my coffee, took my time getting dressed, and spent the rest of the morning simply relaxing. I had taken the day off of work because of a doctor's appointment that afternoon. I remember thinking about the upcoming appointment so casually, and wondering what I would do for the rest of my day off after it was over. It was just a normal day, right up until sixty seconds before my doctor entered the examination room. But sixty seconds after, it became everything BUT an ordinary day, and my life changed forever.

Sixty seconds before, I was still considered "as healthy as a horse," someone who would never imagine in a million years that life could include something so awful—something that only happened to other people—or so I thought. How could it possibly be mine to acquire for an entire lifetime?

Sixty seconds before, I only imagined a future full of tennis matches, camping trips, days spent at the beach, and a little pick-up hockey—I saw myself going on adventurous dates with my husband-to-be who I had not yet met, and as the active mother I had not yet become. I would be the senior who was more active than many teenagers, and the grandmother kicking the ball around in the backyard with my grandchildren.

All of these thoughts only came into focus when I consciously took the time to think about them, and like most twenty-three-year-olds, I rarely thought of the future more than a month in advance, let alone years. Married life and motherhood aside, I didn't need to consciously ponder things like how active I would be, because in my mind it simply went without thinking.

Sixty seconds before my doctor entered the room, I saw myself walking until my very last breath. But sixty seconds after, I was faced with the harsh reality that my future could include something I had never even thought possible: A WHEELCHAIR. Something I had only thought the elderly needed, or people recovering from surgery, an accident, or injury. I had so rarely ever even seen a young person in a wheelchair, and when I had, chronic illness NEVER entered my mind.

As a young woman just recently graduated from university, you don't think of your life involving "chronic" anything. These years were supposed to be for getting a career started, paying off student loans, dating, going to parties, wine tastings, and trips to the yoga studio. The only trips to the doctor's office I had ever made in recent years were for general check-ups, and bladder infections.

Why would I have had any reason to believe it would

be anything more serious on March 18, 2010? I'd be in and out with a referral to the chiropractor—or so I thought. Instead, I was in and out with a prescription to a lifetime of unknowns. Of course, at that point I didn't know what my future held, but not knowing was and continues to be one of the hardest parts. Always wondering how much worse will it get? Will this treatment be my breakthrough? Or how many more tries will it take?

After the usual friendly greeting from my family doctor, it only took him sixty seconds to give me the MRI results that would change my life. What he said versus what I was expecting to hear could not have been any more different. In my mind, the far too persistent numbness in my hands had to be related to one of the multiple hockey injuries I endured in my teenage years. Likely a slipped disc or something similar.

The numbness had gone on for eight months until I could no longer ignore it. It wasn't painful or overly disruptive at that point, it was simply a nuisance—but a nuisance that wouldn't go away. For eight months before my MRI, I went to bed every night hoping that the numbness would just magically disappear on its own, so that I wouldn't have to search for answers I didn't want to consider.

Even after many google searches, I still never thought a chronic illness could be the root cause of some simple numbness, so I continued on with my original thought: hockey injury gone wrong. But sixty seconds after my doctor sat down, it became excruciatingly clear that it was ME who was wrong, and I was no longer your average twenty-three-year-old. I was no longer "as healthy as a horse," and March 18, 2010 was no longer an average day.

Tears immediately welled in my eyes. It didn't take me

long to realize that life as I knew it had just slipped right out of my hands, and this was the "split second" other people talk about when they receive a debilitating diagnosis of their own. I had heard so many times to never take life for granted, because as the tragic stories of others demonstrated, life can change in an instant. This was MY instant, and just like in all the stories I had heard, I never saw it coming. I did not yet understand why or how this would change my life—I just knew this was my new reality, and one that was extremely unwelcome.

I didn't even know what questions to ask my doctor, except one: Is there a cure? I asked this question in hopeful desperation, but already sensed the answer was NO—and I was right.

What else do you ask in a situation like this? The Bomb had been dropped, and my mind, body and soul had just shattered into a million tiny pieces. How was I supposed to compose any type of reasonable response when the air had just been suctioned right out of my lungs, and all I could think of were those two simple yet disastrous words: Multiple Sclerosis (an extremely debilitating auto-immune disorder which causes a number of neurological symptoms. A progressive disease resulting in damage and disruption in both the brain and spinal cord).

I had heard of the illness before, and had even fundraised for it just a few months earlier. I didn't know exactly what it was, but I certainly knew it was far worse than a slipped disc—something which sixty seconds earlier had been the only explanation, quickly vanished into thin air.

"There is no cure, but it is treatable," said my doctor. I still remember those exact words as if it were yesterday. After offering one Kleenex after the next, there was nothing else my doctor could say or do. I left his office as quickly as possible and called my parents, who were on their way to the theatre. Just as shocked as I was, they immediately turned around and arranged for a close family friend to meet me at our house. Although at that point there was absolutely nothing neurologically wrong with my legs, I barely made it up my driveway.

The overwhelming feelings of shock, fear, anger and confusion continued to run rampant not only that evening, but for the months and years to come. I didn't know how to react to the news I had just received. I didn't know what others did in this type of "split second" situation. Did they cry? Reach out for support? Or did they isolate themselves for an indefinite period of time? Did they tell their co-workers, or keep it on the down-low, for fear of losing their job? Did they even care anymore if they had a job at all?

There was no way to know the answers to these questions—I was only twenty-three years old, and these types of problems simply didn't exist in my circle of friends. I can imagine that all of the above scenarios became a reality for some people, but this was my reality and therefore my decision to make. So, I went to bed that night and barely slept, replaying in my mind over and over again the words I had heard just hours ago: "It appears you have Multiple Sclerosis."

Nonetheless, I got up in the morning, went to work and didn't say a single word. I went on with my day as usual, with my new diagnosis lingering in the background of every passing minute. I looked perfectly fine on the outside, but I was a bundle of emotions on the inside. I think I did a pretty good job of holding it together, but make no mistake, one wrong reference and It was cry-fest central.

No matter how hard I tried to act the part, I knew I was far from "normal." A chronic and progressive illness that could potentially rip my world apart at any given instant... It was simply a new part of my life that couldn't and wouldn't be ignored.

As the weeks went on, I continued my research, and every website listed symptoms that sounded so incredibly frightening in their own way: vision loss, spasticity, nerve pain, joint pain, sensory loss, fine and gross motor skill impairment, loss of mobility, coordination issues, memory loss, brain fog, and the list went on... Oh what joy!

But at that point my only symptom was numbness in my hands; a symptom that was not yet disrupting my life or keeping me from playing tennis: my newfound passion. From the moment I made that realization, I considered myself somewhat lucky for the first time since my diagnosis, and decided to continue living my life in the way I loved the most, until the day I no longer could.

CHAPTER TWO

Nothing Routine

JULY 2010

Although I can't remember the exact day of the month, I recall it started off very much like that dreaded day back in March. Nothing fancy or out of the ordinary. It was a Saturday, with a tennis lesson on the calendar.

My father, Ron, had become a member at our home town club in Grimsby, Ontario just a few years before. In fact, he quickly became the President of the club, and remained as such for many years. It's actually a funny story, because my father is SO notorious for being all gung-ho on starting any new fitness endeavor, with his enthusiasm fading fast shortly thereafter. Nonetheless, he constantly talked about how he would love to pick up tennis again, after not playing for over twenty years, and how convenient it would be to play at the Grimsby Tennis Club.

My mother Mary Lou and I were very skeptical of this actually working out, but we bought him a membership for his birthday while secretly rolling our eyes. To make a long story short, he ended up proving us both wrong, and continues to be an active member at not one but two clubs!

A few years after my father joined, he mentioned quite a few times how addictive the sport is and recommended I give it a try. I really had no excuse to not. I was no longer playing hockey or soccer, was still single, didn't yet have the responsibility of children, and I had a stable career working at Great-West Life as an Employee Benefits Specialist. Everything in my life was pretty rock-solid, except for that little thing called MS, lingering over my shoulder.

As the weeks went on and my father became more persistent, I surrendered and decided to give the sport a try. It took me less than an hour on the court to know that tennis and I were meant to spend an entire lifetime together. It was love at first swing! That week I played as much as I possibly could. Being the ultra-competitive person I am, I cannot settle for anything less than my best, and always strive to be the best at anything I try (although I am highly aware this isn't the case!). Even if it wasn't going to happen right away, I wanted to WIN. I wasn't satisfied with just hitting the ball around with my dad. I wanted to compete.

A few weeks after joining the club, I also joined the challenge ladder. Since at this point I had not taken any lessons and had no tactical plan in place, I entered my very first match with one very simple game-plan: get the ball over the net.

I remember frantically running around the court like a wild animal, and relying on my forehand, because my backhand pretty much sucked. BUT I was athletic, which was the only thing keeping me in the match against a member with much more experience.

Two hours later, after a lot of huffing, puffing and extremely awkward-looking shots, I won the match. I was elated to get the win, but also unsatisfied because I knew my technique was far from ideal. I wanted to look good while playing, with at least somewhat proper technique and a general knowledge of tactics. I continued to play matches in the weeks to come, with my same awkward-looking forehand and crappy backhand. I lost more than I won, which only made my competitive edge burn brighter. More than ever, I needed to figure this game out.

A couple months later, my dad decided he wanted to brush up on his own skills and booked a private lesson with our club pro, Joel Cruz. It wasn't long before my father noticed an immense improvement, and needless to say, the lessons continued.

As I persevered with matches of my own, my father continued to notice just how disastrous my backhand really was. It was just as clear to him that something had to be done! Conveniently enough, Joel happened to be at the club every Saturday morning to lead the club's junior program, and quite often got to watch my unorthodox style. My father thought what a great opportunity it would be for a lesson, but it wouldn't wait until then.

I had often seen Joel glancing over to the court where I was playing and wondered what was going through his head. What did he think of my unconventional strokes and my frantic dashes to get the ball over the net just one more time? How did I compare to other beginners he saw playing? Better? Worse? A lost cause? I pondered these unknowns every time he watched me play.

However, I pondered them on an entirely new level on the random day my father asked him to watch me play, and study my backhand. The pressure was on! And just as in most high-pressure situations, the nerves took over and I went from bad to worse. I had never felt more embarrassed playing a sport. It was like I was purposely trying to NOT get the ball over the net.

When the match was over, my father took it a step further and asked Joel if he would mind taking a moment to give me a few pointers. Joel checked his watch and hesitantly agreed. He seemed nervous, but I didn't understand why. Shouldn't I have been the nervous one after absolutely mangling the match? Although it crossed my mind, I doubted I was the worst he had ever taught. He adjusted my racquet a few times and mumbled a few simple instructions. Was this his usual coaching method? I knew he had helped so many others to improve, but surely it took more than just a couple words.

Twenty minutes later, he admitted he was running late for the afternoon session at Niagara Academy of Tennis; a private school incorporating both academics and elite level tennis, where he was a full-time coach. He apologized for having to dash off so quickly, and all I had time to say was thank you!

As the days passed, I kept playing, and I tried to incorporate what I had just learned from Joel into each match: proper grip, racquet preparation and follow through. It looked so effortless when he demonstrated, but when I tried to master it myself, it was anything but.

To anyone who has never played the sport, it is extremely difficult to explain just how frustrating it can be. It looks all "fun and games" from the stands, and a lot of times it is, especially when things are working and you are winning.

The Grimsby Tennis Club is known for its laid-back and friendly atmosphere. Off court, I would agree with that statement one thousand percent. On court, it remains friendly, but there is an additional element added to the mix, as soon as the first serve is in play: competition! No matter how friendly the competition is, it is competition nonetheless, and nobody loves losing.

During the six to seven days a week that I found myself on the court that first summer, I met some pretty outstanding people. People who to this day I consider very close friends. The more time I spent playing with them, the more I got to know their level of competitiveness. Some would self-declare as being ultra-competitive, while others insisted they were not competitive at all. Although I don't believe someone can have absolutely no competitive drive, I do believe that some are just more inclined to having fun on the court regardless of the score.

I always love the days I get to play, but back when I was participating as an able-bodied player, it was often taken for granted. I took for granted just how easy it was to get to the courts on my own, when I wanted and without two wheelchairs. I took for granted just how fun the sport could and should be regardless of the score. I make no excuse for my ultra-competitive self, because at the end of the day, it is such a huge part of my being, both on and off the court. However, I do wish back in that summer of 2010, I had been more able to simply enjoy the moments more purely. I wish I would have taken the time to be both mindful and grateful.

I had already been dealt the cards I wished I had never received, and I did have that mindful moment of considering myself lucky that I had not yet been affected in a worse way. But that moment quickly vanished, and I once again became immersed in trying to live a care-free life. I made that very promise to myself when I decided what I would do post-diagnosis: continue living life as normally as I could. I thought that by trying to push the diagnosis out of my mind, that maybe I would also push it out of my body.

If I was overly content with my tennis progression and simply loved each and every day on the court regardless of my performance, the burning desire to become better would not have existed, and I never would have found such a crucial missing piece of the puzzle. That piece being my first planned lesson with Joel.

As I mentioned, I started off the day as usual, with optimistic expectations for the upcoming lesson. The lesson was semi-private and split with my father. At forty-five dollars an hour, they were certainly more appealing when shared! I showed up right on time, looking the part with my "on point" tennis attire and eagerness to learn. I was totally ready to leave my sucky backhand in the dust, and for that lesson to be the beginning of a new and improved player.

The first thing I noticed about Joel was his genuine nature. I had an inkling about this from having watched him coach other players, and also due to the fact he was booked solid every evening of the week and weekends. For this to happen, it was clear people liked him. I guessed it was likely due to much more than his stellar coaching skills. After all, from my time spent working in sales, I knew that regardless of the product or service being sold, people buy from people.

Joel greeted us with a vibrant smile, one I had seen many times before, even from three courts away. He asked us what we wanted to focus on, and when we both responded with "everything," he put us to work immediately. He knew there was a lot of work to do even more than we did. It quickly became apparent through his comments, that he had been watching us more than we had thought. It seemed he had this innate ability to see what we were doing wrong from a distance, while staying focused on his own court. This was confirmed in the weeks to come, when he would make statements about how well I had played that day, when I hadn't seen him glance over at my court even once. Just when I thought he wasn't looking, he most definitely was!

Like rapid fire, my father and I began hitting forehands and backhands, and then switched when requested by Joel. Although he appeared to be a really nice guy, once the lesson started, he meant business. With the balls coming at us faster than we could manage, we finished the large basket of balls within minutes, and the pick-up process began. It was in this very moment, four months post-diagnosis, that everything changed, and I knew the lesson would never again be merely routine.

CHAPTER THREE

No Time Wasted

SUMMER 2010

"So what university did you attend?" asked Joel. Seconds earlier, we had confirmed we had both attended post-secondary institutions. It was the first topic of conversation we broached that wasn't related to tennis. "Brock University, for Sports Management," I answered. I later learned that Joel was surprised to hear I had already graduated from Brock, since he thought I was quite a few years younger than him.

As we continued to pick up the balls that were scattered all over the court, I learned that Joel was originally from Oaxaca, Mexico where his family still resided, that he had recently graduated from Niagara College with a Sales and Marketing Diploma, and most importantly, that his name was only spelled like Joel but pronounced like ho-el. Think "Noel" but with an H.

How embarrassing! All this time my father and I had both been mispronouncing his name, yet he still responded every single time. Turns out we were the only members at the club who were aware of the proper pronunciation, as he had willingly surrendered to the Canadian version of his name.

The ball picking up process took at least five minutes longer than it should have that day, as we both fell deeper into curious conversation. Within the extra few minutes, I learned that Joel had only been in Canada for ten years and that he came on a Tennis Scholarship to Niagara Academy of Tennis. I also discovered that he came from a modest background and that he had not spoken a single word of English when he arrived in Canada.

I was instantly intrigued by Joel and his story thus far. I wanted to learn more—but we had a lesson to finish, and my father was probably wondering what was taking us so long. We wrapped up the lesson forty-five minutes later, and in that instant, everything I saw in Joel changed. I no longer saw him solely as a fantastic tennis coach with a genuine demeanor and a vibrant smile. For the first time since we met during that semi-awkward twenty-minute lesson, I needed to know more—not more about how to correct my tennis technique, but about his story.

What was it like to move away from his entire family for so many years? He mentioned that he had just gotten back a couple days ago from visiting his family, but did he have the opportunity to visit often? How did his mother feel knowing that she would no longer get to see him every day? Did he have any siblings? How difficult was it for him to become accustomed to Canadian culture? And most importantly, was he planning on staying in Canada?

These were just a few of the many questions running through my mind, and I knew getting answers would take time. They were questions that could not be answered during a quick break in our next lesson. But the craziest thought to enter my mind was on the fate of my future.

For reasons unknown, I found myself thinking that Joel would likely make a great husband. Someone who would be loving, caring, respectful and loyal. It absolutely blew my mind how I could have these thoughts after one miniscule conversation, but it simply was what it was. I thought about it more than once, and at that point all I could do was make sure I didn't say it out loud!

That same evening I had a match against a male member of our club. I obviously wanted to win but also realized it would be a tough task. So rather than obsessing over a victory, I obsessed over focusing on the adjusted forehand and backhand I had learned just a few hours earlier.

The match went as expected and although I was not the winner on the scoreboard, I was extremely happy with how I played and was proud of myself for incorporating much of what I had learned. Even though the match didn't end until after nine, I felt I needed to share the news and immediately thought of Joel. I didn't know if he would be receptive to me texting him so late and after-hours, if after-hours even existed for a tennis coach?

From what I had seen, Joel could be found teaching a group or private lesson at almost every hour of the day or evening. But all I knew in that moment was that he wasn't at the courts THAT evening, which added to my hesitation before sending the message. Even if he didn't mind, would he care? Or would he just think I was some sort of stalker student who had a major obsession with the game? But with an almost immediate response back, it was crystal clear that he, too, was open to an "after-hours" convo. The curiosity of who Joel was as a person off the courts continued to flood my mind, and I was hopeful that he may have had even the slightest bit of curiosity about me too.

After our next lesson lasted three hours, it was obvious that the connection was real, and this potential love story was off to the races before either of us could comprehend. Were my strange thoughts of marriage not so strange at all? After our marathon of a lesson, we went our separate ways and while we both new that crushes were blooming, who would make the next move was still unknown.

Turns out it was him!

That evening, he asked me to go for a drink at a local pub, and although he never used the word "date," I felt it highly unlikely that he was so committed to his coaching career, that he would go out after-hours to solely discuss the technical improvements of my forehand. It was possible it may be a topic of conversation, but surely not the sole purpose for the "get-together."

This was the opportunity I had been waiting for. The chance to really get to know where his down to earth essence stemmed from, and the chance to ask a couple of those looming questions I had in mind. To say I was excited would be an understatement. I couldn't quite understand just what the feelings were all about, but I knew I had never felt them before—a level of calm once around him, but also the butterflies beforehand.

I got so caught up in the moment, that for the first time since that fateful day in March 2010, I forgot I was different than your average twenty-three-year-old. Despite the tingling in my hands that remained an ongoing nuisance, I actually forgot I had MS.

We continued to see each other almost every day at the courts, and although we tried to keep things on the down-low, that didn't last for long. Our typical three-hour lessons continued on a regular basis, and the members who had not yet caught onto our budding romance probably thought I was either getting a great deal OR I was made of money. It was definitely NOT the latter!

As the weeks progressed, so did our relationship. We continued our tennis lessons, but also spent a lot of time together off-court. My family and our close tennis friends had their suspicions confirmed, and we received an outpouring of love and support. I also was relieved to become an official couple, since the forty-five-dollar lessons were WAY beyond my budget.

With each and every passing day, we began to learn more and more about each other, and in particular what it was that ingrained into us the drive and determination we both shared. He was so modest that he didn't quite see why anyone would be interested in hearing his story. Little did he know, he was SO very wrong. And for me, I was raised by two extremely strong parents, so I always owed it to them for any drive or determination I had built.

That being said, we were both still considered relatively young, with a lot of growing left to do. As much as I liked to think I was a person of firm resolve and bravery, I never knew what bravery could really entail. If only I could have seen into the future and understood the storm that was coming my way, I may have been more grateful, and a lot more prepared.

But even so, would anything have changed? Or does the REAL change only occur after being slammed with multiple levels of adversity? At twenty-three, even after being diagnosed with one of the most chronically debilitating illnesses to exist, there was no way I could have even begun to entertain the depth of those thoughts.

On our third date, I mustered the courage to tell Joel that I was recently diagnosed with MS, and did my best to describe the type of disability that could occur. However, as he has recently put it, I looked normal. He couldn't feel the tingling in my fingertips, which no matter how hard I tried to ignore, was just enough to remind me that I was far from normal. But how were either of us realistically supposed to back out of a relationship we both desperately wanted, simply out of a fear for the unknown?

The short answer is we COULDN'T

Four months later, on Christmas Eve 2010, we got engaged, and a year and half after that, on June 9, 2012, I became MRS. Gillian Cruz. We did it! But it was not nearly as effortless as it may have appeared.

It wasn't until I could no longer swing a racquet, when I really began to understand the type of disruption MS could cause. Almost exactly a year later, the one thing that had brought Joel and I together, became only ONE of the things we could no longer do.

Aside from tennis and other sports, the tingling in my right hand and arm advanced to the point that I could no longer do the everyday type of tasks, such as buttoning up my shirt, writing my own name, or opening my own water bottle. I could no longer feed myself properly, dry my own hair, or even fill out my own disability claim.

I found myself constantly researching how long typical flare ups lasted, and with each and every passing month, I got closer to the deadline. It wasn't until six months later that I slowly regained function. In early years of diagnosis, most MS patients have what is referred to as Relapsing Remitting Multiple Sclerosis (RRMS). This entails times of relapses lasting anywhere from a few days to a year, and no one knows when or where they will strike.

These times of relapses, or flare-ups, are then followed by an eventual remission, and the hope is that the majority of function will be regained. Unfortunately this doesn't always happen. In the instance of the flare up in my arm, I did regain most function, but I still have days that my fine motor skills aren't quite on-point and a greater level of weakness may persist. The numbness also remains a part of the new me. Although I was happy to regain about eighty-five percent of function, I also became extremely frightened about the unknowns of my future.

With my recovery after the flare up so recent, the unknowns of my future continued to plague my mind. Questions such as: will this be the worst it will get? Should I be grateful, or more worried than ever before? How relentless can and will this illness become?

I already had heard from many people that the course of MS for each individual is very different. There are no two MS patients who can totally relate to one another. I had already decided in my mind that losing my mobility would be the worst-case scenario, but knew this was more uncommon than not. Although I couldn't help but imagine how devastating this scenario would be, I tried to push it out of my mind as I crossed my fingers and toes that I would not be the minority. After all, I was now an engaged woman and I had a wedding to plan.

Joel and I decided to opt for a year and a half engagement and felt that having a longer engagement would be beneficial for two reasons. Number one being the obvious, that it would give us more time to plan, and number two, we had wasted no time in putting a ring on it. I say "we" because we were both completely on-board with getting engaged so quickly, and we had multiple discussions about the timing. I knew it was going to happen soon, I just didn't know the exact date. Like tennis, we were both convinced we were destined to spend a lifetime together.

We had both recently gotten out of five-year relationships, and although we both held great respect for our exes, the relationships weren't progressing. We both wanted more, and we found it in each other. Our chemistry was undeniable and we had similar interests. That being said, we were different in many ways. I was more a social butterfly while he was a homebody. He loved movie nights in his comfy off-court clothing, while I couldn't wait to either host or be hosted by close friends. I never was a huge party animal, as I found clubs and bars very claustrophobic. I had gone to them in my recent university years, but more as a way to stay social since it was the thing to do.

But once the university years ended, so did my nights out at all of the regular weekend spots. I became more in love with tennis than any bar, and my circle of friends changed immensely.

Yes, Joel and I overcame the only level of adversity we knew thus far as a couple, but we were far from prepared for the continuous chain of unfortunate events yet to occur. The level of adversity we once considered challenging quickly vanished into thin air, only left to be yearned for, and we rapidly found ourselves fighting a war we for so long had assumed would NEVER happen to us. A war that was never ending, with many battles left to be conquered.

As I look back at that time in my life nearly eight years ago, it is hard to remember all the details, but all that really matters now is the realization that the worst level of awful we know is the one we've experienced. I wish more than anything that my level of awful ended there... Experiencing what it was like to be dependent, disabled, and unable to play the one sport I loved, but then regaining all of it back and left feeling more grateful than ever before. However, THAT, to this day, remains a distant memory, and the level of awful I so badly wish I could gain back.

CHAPTER FOUR

Work Life Worries

(PRE-DIAGNOSIS, JUNE 2009)

I was stable in my career at Great-West Life as an Employee Benefits Specialist, but the commute was certainly a downside. I was lucky to be hired so quickly only two months after graduating and originally started my career in Kitchener Ontario, with an hour-and-a-half commute. My very first interview for the job was in Hamilton Ontario, and I wasn't aware they were also hiring for Kitchener. Hamilton would have been a better commute—only twenty-five minutes away—but I was offered Kitchener, and didn't even hesitate before accepting. With my father being a retired principal and my mother a retired teacher, I had always been taught the value in gaining access into the workforce, even if it's not an ideal position.

I ended up loving my coworkers, and found the transition into my new role generally seamless. Only two weeks after starting, I was required to attend a four-week training session at the Great-West Life headquarters in Winnipeg. It was certainly difficult to be away from home, but I was extremely grateful it was not in the winter!

Shortly after my return from Winnipeg, my current boss offered me an opportunity that had just opened up. There was a new opening for the exact same role in Mississauga. I would have a shorter distance commute, but also a whole lot of traffic. Either way, the time spent driving was not going to change much, and regardless, I sensed I didn't really have a choice. It was one of those opportunities you had just better take.

Just weeks later, I found myself at a new cubicle, in a new city, and surrounded by a new bunch of coworkers. It was a bigger office for sure, with generally more demanding clients. I chalk that up to the hustle and bustle of the territory, with a more formal atmosphere and often a heightened stress load. To add to the stress of the change in location and in pace, I decided to part ways with my boyfriend of five years, and while I was confident in my decision, I knew it was going to be tough to say goodbye to that segment of my journey.

But life went on...

I became more and more accustomed to my new location, and I quickly built a backbone stronger than ever before. This little thing called sassiness, or maybe even attitude, started to bloom as misogynist assholes pissed me off. Don't get me wrong—there were many friendly clients and co-workers who entered my world in my new territory, but the change also came with some not so pleasant ones. The people who would make you think to yourself "Are you for real?!" The ones who would make that little bit of sassiness soar and the ones who would make your ability to hang up the phone that much easier.

Without a doubt, working as an Employee Benefits Specialist in the Greater Toronto Area (GTA) served me well.

My confidence flourished, as did my knowledge in sales, customer service, and knowing when to say NO. I arrived at the office in Mississauga as a shy girl new to her career, and three-and-a-half years later I left as an independent career woman on a mission: to build my own business as a Financial Advisor.

CHAPTER FIVE

A Needed Change

NOVEMBER 2011

Deciding to alter my career path was not easy. I waffled back and forth for almost a year before I gained the courage necessary to make the move. As an Employee Benefits Specialist, I was being paid a decent base salary, but it rarely exceeded that. There were team bonus opportunities available, but they were very difficult to hit.

The role itself included developing group benefits plans for businesses, but we were considered the middle men doing a solid portion of the work, and often presenting quotations on behalf of the Financial Advisors. In essence, we did most of the work and the Financial Advisors got paid. In the first couple years of my career, I was okay with this. I knew it would be a very challenging task to become a Financial Advisor and work solely on commissioned income. But I had to try. I had visions of growing my career in the insurance industry, and building my own empire of clients.

It made sense for my plan to include focusing on businesses looking for group benefits, and to branch out into

Life and Living benefits as I built up my block of business. It seemed like a great plan, even when having that annoying tingling in my arms. For over a year it remained just that—a plan. I continued on as a single woman with a solid career, but a career that was not my passion. I never really thought that life as a Financial Advisor would fill that void either, but I thought it would be a welcomed change and challenge.

I thought about it almost every day, and had a few meetings with the recruitment director at London Life. If I were to make this change, I would become a London Life Financial Advisor as well as a Mutual Fund Consultant. It sounded pretty fancy, but also overwhelming. Going from a comfortable base salary to the unknowns of commission was actually quite terrifying. Yet still, I was confident I would one day make it happen. What I didn't realize, was all the stress I was accumulating by simply thinking about making the step, rather than actually taking it.

In the midst of all my personal stress, unknowns and indecisiveness, Joel's career remained consistent. Due to the nature of his job, Joel worked long shifts generally starting at seven in the morning and ending at nine o'clock at night. During the early years of our engagement, my MS presented itself as challenging in many ways, but manageable. We both had full-time careers without the responsibility of a child or a mortgage. I knew Joel was so passionate about coaching, that all the long hours and nights with sore feet were worth it to him. Seeing how much he loved his career made it difficult for either of us to discuss a change. He did have that handy diploma in Sales and Marketing, which I knew would become very useful one day. In fact, Joel had mentioned before that he knew he would one day have to make a switch. But up until that point, he was in a completely different line of work. One that embodied his passion, with a ten-minute drive and a more relaxed atmosphere. We were different people, in different careers, with very different stories. Through this, we found each other intriguing and even when the days were tough, we found a way to become tougher and to never let the bad days win.

Up until this point, I never really took the time to think about what shaped us into the couple we became, but I would definitely place overcoming adversity at the very top of the list.

Even on the days when I couldn't swing a racquet, we tried our best to find other things in common and sought other ways to be happy together. EVEN after I had already been dealt my diagnosis, I never gave up on my plan to become a Financial Advisor, and more importantly, Joel's support never wavered. But just before I made my biggest career move yet, tragedy struck...

In September 2012, my aunt Kathy (Kate) Gilchrist, whom I was very close to, tragically passed away. Even when she lived on the other side of the country, she stayed in close contact and knew all about my new endeavors. Needless to say, this was devastating for my entire family. Although she left this world much too soon, I am grateful she was able to attend my wedding in 2012, just months before her passing. In respect for the sensitive details of this tragedy, I will leave it as that—a tragedy. It took a long time to come to grips with the fact that she was gone and I would never have the chance to see her again.

Inevitably, my emotional and physical stress increased to a level my body could no longer handle. It was a slow and steady build up, having undergone three major shifts in my life, all within three years: a change in job locations, an intense break up, and the tragic loss of my aunt. At that time, I never realized the level of chaos this caused, particularly as it related to my MS.

But now I can tell you with 100% certainty, it led to the most debilitating attack I have ever had, and the one that has entirely changed my life. I never knew what adversity could really entail, or what being strong REALLY meant.

CHAPTER SIX

Downhill Slide

NOVEMBER 2012

Just two months after my aunt passed away, my health started to really deteriorate. I never wanted to fully admit that it was happening to me, so I pushed on and ignored all the times I tripped over my own two feet. I ignored the increased heaviness in my limbs and chalked it up to a build up of lactic acid, as a result of too many tennis matches. But in the back of my mind, I knew it was the MS making itself known.

The tripping wasn't often enough for me to hang up my racquet for the second time, but it was certainly disruptive. When my mind would wander into the dark visions of a wheelchair, I purposefully played more tennis. I thought that maybe I just needed to become more mindful of my feet and where they were in space. I also thought that perhaps I just needed to strengthen my muscles, and the tripping would become a non-issue.

As it turns out, I couldn't have been more wrong in every sense. The casual tripping turned into a more regular thing, to the point where it became more frustrating to play than to not. It was time to call a spade a spade and recognize I was going downhill faster than I could fathom. Numbness had rapidly taken over my entire leg a while back, but by November 2012, it had gone from disruptive to debilitating. Just like during the flare up in my arm, the fine and gross motor skills were not responding in their usual fashion.

In September, although my leg was numb, I could still go on walking fairly normally, and unless someone was fixated on my movement, they would likely not notice anything overly alarming. It is absolutely mind-boggling how much something can change in a mere two months, whether it's the weather, a friend, a sport, or an illness... if there is one thing I learned back in 2010, 2011, and 2012, it is that change can happen in the blink of an eye. We can be cruising along in life feeling good, looking good, and acting the part, but no matter how hard we try or how good we feel, sometimes it's just not enough.

CHAPTER SEVEN

Like It Was Yesterday

On a Wednesday night in November 2012, I was asked to spare in a men's mixed doubles night. By this point, I had improved enough to play with and against the men, and often got asked to fill in when they were short on numbers. My dad also played in this league, and it was always a great night for us both.

However, on this particular Wednesday, something was different. I didn't accept the invitation to play with the same degree of enthusiasm as usual. I had no longer been able to play at my regular pace for a few weeks. I didn't want to admit this fact to myself, so I just kept pushing on, and watched myself giving up on balls I would normally return, and saying "nice shot" to my opponent far more often. Up until this point, I was known mostly for being quick on my feet and my ability to run balls down. Ironically, I was known for my mobility.

But not anymore—my biggest strength was rapidly becoming my biggest weakness. In fact, I'm not even sure if I could convincingly state I could even run at all anymore. More accurately, I was down to a swift speed-walk. My balance was still in decent order, but it was such a task to move in any urgent manner. Even picking up the ball between points became an unwanted responsibility.

It was such a surreal feeling, to lose the ability to move my legs the right way, and to move in mere slow-motion. On that Wednesday, I couldn't comprehend exactly what was happening, I just knew that things were worse than normal. Literally, up until I started playing that evening, I could move more freely. Yes, the feeling of weights being strapped to my right leg still existed, but with no alternative, I managed it. It was absolutely frightening that I was swiftly losing the game I loved for the second time.

I pushed through the evening of tennis, and anyone with even the slightest level of observation knew I was not okay, but very few people knew I had MS. I just sort of felt it unnecessary to go around telling everybody about my invisible diagnosis. I just thought it would look like an invitation to a personal pity party. Until there were any visible signs of anything gone wrong, what was I supposed to say? "Oh hey, just so you know, I have a touch of MS (short for Multiple Sclerosis), but so far so good!"

There were simply no words that would make that conversation any easier, so avoidance became the ticket. In the month or two leading up to that Wednesday in November, I was able to pass off any stumble, trip, or ankle roll as merely fatigue and say I was clumsy by nature. But there could only be so many of those moments before minds began to wonder. My close friends at the club knew my situation, but the Wednesday night group of men had no clue.

As with much of my story, my tennis demise became a reality during one oh so simple moment. The type of moment that could have happened at any given time, before or after. But for whatever reason, it occurred on that Wednesday evening, when I tried to move faster than my body allowed in a desperate attempt to make it to a drop shot.

My right knee gave out in a weird hyperextension kind of way and I stumbled to the ground. The strangest part is it didn't even hurt, yet the tears still poured out. From anyone else's perspective, they had just seen an injury, like so many others had experienced. It wasn't until the moment I was hobbling off the court that I announced I had Multiple Sclerosis, NOT an injury. I still remember that evening like it was yesterday.

Although I was beyond devastated knowing this was not something that would get better overnight, I still held hope that it wouldn't be too long before I regained my ability to play once again. I reminisced about the first time MS took tennis away from me, and remembered how hard it was to just simply watch. I recalled how difficult it was to continuously wonder how long the flare up would last, and how many months I'd have to endure it.

I remembered being on disability for six months due to my first flare-up, unable to do everyday tasks with my hand, and wondering why I had to have one of the longer flare ups. Why couldn't I be like almost everyone else in the MS world and have a flare up lasting only a couple weeks or a few months at most? I also remember being grateful to eventually regain the amount of function I did, and not knowing what I would have done if I hadn't.

And in a blink of an eye, there I was two years later, going through the exact same thought process, only about a different body part. I wondered if I would once again have a long flare up lasting six months, or if I would be luckier this time. But as the months continued to tick on by, I became increasingly worried and impatient. When it passed the six-month mark, I wondered why. I still didn't know all too much about the illness, but I was sure I had read that almost all flare ups didn't extend past this timeframe. Still, I remained that optimistic person who didn't think I would be the exception to the rule.

I was NEVER very lucky. I never won anything. Except for some reason I was lucky enough to land this horrific life-altering beast of an illness. The saying "If it weren't for bad luck I wouldn't have any luck at all" sure rang loud and true in this regard.

But wasn't this enough? Wasn't it enough to now always be known as the girl with MS? No matter how many other qualities people would see in me first, and no matter what positive feelings they may have about me, I'd still be the girl with MS. Why did I then ALSO have to become the girl with MS with horrible luck? The girl who continues to fight every day to gain back multiple parts of her life without any luck. The girl who never gives up, who always looks for the next avenue of attack, yet STILL no luck.

BAD luck was what I saw and felt in my life for a very, very, very long time. Has my luck gotten any better? I guess that's open to interpretation, and I'll let you be the judge of that in future chapters. But for now, let's see what happened after that evening of tennis back in November 2012.

From that very last moment on the courts, everything got worse, slowly but surely. I went from having my right leg and torso affected, to also having my left leg join the party not too long after. Not only did I now have my entire body from my chest down burdened by numbness, but I also had the terrible suffocating feelings of tightness, heaviness, rigidness, and worst of all NERVE PAIN- The feeling of being burnt in a fire, or sometimes it was more like being frostbitten or stung by an entire swarm of bees. The sensations can best be described as TORTURE.

Most people do their best to understand what widespread chronic nerve pain is all about, but with no disrespect, unless you have lived even a single day with this god-awful pain, you really don't know. Reading about it versus experiencing it are not the same. Doctors have admitted it is the most difficult type of pain to treat, and hearing that doesn't make you feel too confident that much can be done. Over the past seven years of battling through this debilitating pain, I have unfortunately come to realize I was right. There ISN'T anything that helps much more than "Surface Level." I have no doubt that there are others who benefit from nerve pain medications or therapies more than I do, but this is my journey and my experiences.

When I say I have tried everything, I have tried everything I have come across to date. Every pain medication, lidocaine infusions, Chinese medicine, naturopathic therapies, different diets, massage therapy, meditation, yoga, medical marijuana, TENS device, etc. etc. etc.

The pain was not too disruptive at first, more of just a nuisance slightly worse than the nuisance in my hand back in 2010. But month by month it got worse, and once again, I felt a total loss of control over my own body, as if it were an object slipping right out of my hands. It wasn't until 2014 when the pain started to become so severe that I then considered it my most debilitating symptom, winning the prize over my loss of mobility. Just when I thought I knew what my worst nightmare was, I was proven SO incredibly wrong.

CHAPTER 8

My Darkest Days

MARCH 2013

During the months and even years before the pain really hit, I was still a hot mess. I lost all ability to not only run, but to also walk in any normal way and without debilitating fatigue. I would stand up with my legs shaking beneath me, and my body would immediately tighten from a neurological disruption. The type of disruption that sooner or later becomes the nemesis for all MS warriors. It is one of the most difficult and unusual feelings to explain, but it is basically like being in vice grips, getting tighter second by second.

The feeling of paralysis would take over, and I couldn't take a step forward without grabbing onto something sturdy in front of me and gasping for air. Whether it be a hand to grab, a table to steady myself, a wall to lean against, or my own cane, I was no longer able to walk with ease or independence and it shattered me both physically and emotionally.

It became a near impossible task to walk a few feet to the bathroom or to get a glass of water. Even with the walls always available for support, it was generally not enough. Almost every time I would try to walk, I would cry. I would break down knowing this was not a temporary thing. I would hear over and over again in my head, "It appears you have Multiple Sclerosis." The words "chronic illness" played on repeat in my mind and I could NOT believe this was my life. I spent many hours of many days wondering what I did to deserve this, and every month that went by without regaining any function, more resentment and down-right anger built up.

I thought of all the people in this world who did absolutely awful things to others, and wondered why they couldn't be the ones burdened with this gut-wrenching life sentence. I thought of all the criminals who were given a simple five-year jail sentence, and thought an MS diagnosis would have been a far more fitting punishment. Something that would REALLY change their lives and make them think twice before ever taking their own or another's independence or freedom for granted.

I went through a long period of time, probably a few years, when Facebook became a platform which did far more harm than good for my mental state. It became a place that reminded me of not only the person I no longer was, but acted as the perfect platform for resentment. I was jealous of everyone else who could still live their lives however they wanted. Every time I saw a picture of young women dressed up in heels, old friends playing soccer, or mothers looking like "Super Moms," my heart would shatter a little bit more.

It was never because I wished ill on anyone else. It was merely because I once had everything they had, and wanted nothing more than to have it all back. Even if I hadn't yet become a mother myself, my dreams of the mother I knew I would never become were shattered. Even if I hadn't yet been married long enough to know how drastically our lives as husband and wife would change, I had vivid images of the co-ed soccer we wouldn't play, the tennis tournaments in which we would no longer participate, and the brisk walks we no longer take. You see, that's one of the craziest parts about MS. It can make you lose so much before it's even gone.

As the months and years ticked by, nothing ever got easier, only more exhausting. Not only did simple tasks become more cumbersome from a physical standpoint, but also from a mental standpoint, continuously being reminded of all that I had lost, all I hadn't gained back, and all the days ahead I'd be forced to endure. I began to play the "grass is always greener on the other side" game, and wondered why I was one way and not the other.

For instance, during the earliest days of my impaired mobility, I wondered why MS had to pick on this aspect of my life, knowing how active a person I was. As my mobility continued to worsen to the point I could no longer take those mere few steps, I literally said out loud that pain would be better, because at least I could push through that. Then once I became burdened with BOTH pain and impaired mobility, I realized just how idiotic my thoughts had been. I suddenly wished I could take back everything I had said, and still yearn for the days when I ONLY had impaired mobility.

I would obsess over the people on Facebook who I THOUGHT had it all, and would get straight up pissed off when they would complain about their runny nose or the WHOLE week they were down and out with the flu. I couldn't understand why people posted messages as if their life was over, because of a missed job opportunity or a fight with a best friend.

There were people looking for a pity party for an upcoming surgery on a limb—something that would at least heal. I often was angry at the fact that they couldn't see how much worse someone in my situation had it, and wondered why they couldn't see it that way.

I didn't understand why people felt it necessary to ramble on social media about first-world problems, when there were others who actually had REAL problems that would never go away. I felt it insensitive for people to complain about their job and how much it sucked getting up early for work when, one: It was NEVER easy for me to get up at all, and two: Working was one of the things I quickly lost the ability to do.

Not surprisingly, the resentment I felt drifted over to the tennis club, and once again I found myself frustrated and feeling angry over the fact that I couldn't play, as well as towards those who COULD play but still found reasons to complain.

At the beginning of year two (2014), being unable to play tennis, I decided to volunteer on the Grimsby Tennis Club Executive as the Tournament Director. Although mentally and emotionally difficult, I still thought it would be a good way of staying involved in the sport. It was also the summer I got pregnant, and I used that to justify to myself that I wouldn't be able to play anyways.

Not only was I responsible for organizing the tournaments, but I also took on the role of running both the Ladies Doubles Night and the Mixed Doubles Night. This involved setting up matches in the round robins, and changing those match-ups every twenty-five minutes. It involved creating well balanced teams, incorporating beginners into the mix, and trying my best to ensure everyone had a great experience.

A lot of nights were difficult since there was often an uneven number and sometimes too many players, with someone having to sit out each round. It was always a balancing act which I had to make look seamless, and there was hardly ever an evening that went without a complaint.

Whether it was during the tournaments or during the doubles nights, there was always at least one person who wasn't happy. It was impossible to please everyone, and despite doing my best every time, there was almost always someone who felt it was not enough. Don't get me wrong—most members expressed their appreciation and commented on how well-run the events were. I appreciated getting this feedback, and it motivated me to persevere until the end of the season.

However, my blood boiled when I received feedback such as: there were too many matches, or there were not enough matches, or I played with him too many times, or I wanted to play with the better players more, or I had to play too early, or the tournament ran too late, or it was too hot to play in the middle of the day, or it was too cold to have an outdoor tournament at that time of year, or the divisions should have played on separate weekends, or it would have been better to have everything done on two days not three, or merely complaining that their knee was hurting because of overuse (and me thinking, whose fault was that?).

At the beginning of the season I was better able to disregard those types of comments, but once I had invested three or four months of my time every week at league nights, and put many hours into organizing tournaments, it became increasingly more difficult to simply ignore. Rather than just thinking to myself, "be grateful you can play at all," I verbalized it.

41

I simply couldn't hold back my resentment and inability to comprehend how and why some people just couldn't see how much of a gift it was, every single time they stepped onto the court. I just couldn't understand why they were taking for granted the one thing I so desperately wanted back. Why on earth could they look me in the eyes and complain that they were scheduled for too MANY matches, when I would give anything I had just to play one.

I really did believe that by staying close to the tennis club, I would feel like I was still a player. Perhaps by running tournaments, I would play vicariously through other members—but it was far from that. It was hardest for me to organize and watch the Women's division, as I knew I should have been out there with them. It was even worse when I watched the Women's Singles tournament, as it was always my favourite. I had played with the top member in the Women's division many times, and we would often split matches. It was always a toss up whether it would be her or me who would win, and I missed those matches and compe-tition immensely.

Although it became increasingly more heartbreaking as the months went on, I had always been taught to never back out of a commitment, so on I went. Throughout my entire time on the GTC Executive, as well as the many months I spent feeling resentment and jealousy towards others, I eventually began to reflect on the entire situation. I became more aware of why people made Facebook posts about what I considered to be first world problems. I became better able to understand why people would speak about the burden work was to them, or why a fight with their best friend was a time in their life they just couldn't snap out of.

Through further reflection, I found answers to why

some people weren't more grateful for the little things in their lives, and why they took the simple ability to walk for granted. For the first time since the loss of myself, I found peace in realizing why people didn't consider themselves lucky when being dealt with a problem they could fix, or an injury from which they could heal.

I FINALLY understood why the reality they were facing was the only reality they felt, and why they didn't, and couldn't comprehend what life was like as an 'MSer'. Once known, the answer seemed so simple, yet still something that took me a long time to fully acknowledge. It was the brutal truth, that the only version of awful we know, is the one we are experiencing or have experienced. And furthermore, our WORST version of awful is only as bad as our WORST experience.

"BRAVER THAN YOUR BATTLE"
Blog Excerpt
"The Multiple in Multiple Sclerosis"
July 19, 2017

Over the past multiple years of learning how to live with all that is MS and navigating through life as the new me, I have come to the conclusion that the "Multiple" in Multiple Sclerosis means MUCH more than the obvious "Multiple Scars" or "Multiple Lesions"...

It's learning how to deal with the multiple curve-balls thrown your way and being forced to see life in multiple different ways.

It's feeling multiple emotions on multiple days and managing them despite sometimes feeling a total loss of control.

It's feeling multiple symptoms, at multiple severities and trying multiple therapies in the hopes of easing them.

It's asking and answering multiple questions asked in multiple different ways on multiple different days.

It's dreading the multiple times you will have to get up to go to the bathroom, kitchen, answer the door, or any other task that drains your energy in ways which at some point seemed incomprehensible.

It's the multiple times you will lose your balance, appear drunk while walking, lose your ability to walk at all, trip over absolutely nothing, or take a FULL out ROCK hard fall...and THEN the MULTIPLE times you will get back up and shake it all off.

It's the multiple times you will say "It's Neurological, NOT muscular," and the multiple times you will ask yourself when that powerful brain of yours will wake back up.

It's the multiple moments you will choose to embrace the cards you've been dealt, and then the multiple more moments you will want to scream at the top of your lungs!

It's the multiple, multiple, MULTIPLE times you will try to do something you know you can't do, JUST to see if anything has changed.

It's the debilitating fatigue that overwhelms your body JUST from doing one of the MULTIPLE tasks, which at one point seemed SO second nature.

It's the multiple degrees of pain you feel and the multiple words used to try to describe it, but that just don't do it justice.

It's the multiple times you feel let down when a treatment fails to relieve your symptoms, and then the multiple new ones you immediately start researching.

It's trying to picture the multiple little aliens that have taken a hold of your body, and envisioning all the multiple ways of defeating them.

It's ALL of the multiple challenges you fight on a daily basis due to an incurable chronic beast that is OFTEN too afraid to show its face.

It's taking pride in recognizing the multiple battles you've already won, yet continuously preparing yourself for the NEVER ending WAR.

It's finding a balance between all your multiple melt-downs, and trying to remain that strong, positive and courageous person deep within.

It's being thankful for the multiple people who love, support and encourage you through your ever winding journey, and not being able to picture going through it without them.

It's recognizing the multiple layers of resilience you have already built, and anticipating the multiple new ones yet to develop.

BUT MOST IMPORTANTLY...

It's NEVER letting the multiple layers of adversity outweigh the MULTIPLE triumphs and successes you've endured.

Because one day, I truly believe that all of these "multiple" things will come to ONE happy ending, and we will ALL be able to say:

"I USED to have Multiple Sclerosis...but that was MULTIPLE years ago!"

CHAPTER NINE

Turning Tables

Although there was that period of time when I felt irritation towards those complaining about things which seemed so trivial, I now realize that to the person knocked out for a week with a debilitating flu, it really WAS awful. If that person had never experienced anything more awful than the flu, it would be harder for them to understand just how much worse their situation could be. The fight between best friends really did cause a terrible strain on their relationship, and perhaps they had never experienced a feud worse than that. And the person complaining about how much of a burden work was to them, quite possibly never experienced the loss of their ability to work at all.

It all comes down to one simple truth that we all know, yet are often unable to truly grasp until we are faced with an ultimate loss. That truth being, that we all take the simple things in life for granted until we no longer have them. Most of us can admit how much worse another person's reality is, yet we still never think it will happen to us. Even though we know other people are struggling just to live, we are quickly sucked back into our own reality, because we simply do not live in theirs.

This doesn't mean we are not sympathetic, empathetic, or compassionate people, yet simply means we aren't them and have never walked a day in their shoes. Understandably, we only have momentary glimpses of their lives before we must resume our own. From my own personal experiences, I have seen so many others fighting battles I would NEVER wish to be mine, and although I now take more time to stop and recognize this, it doesn't make my own battle any easier. I continue to feel pain, fatigue, immobility, loss of sensation, and so many other debilitating symptoms, but unlike before, I now hold more gratitude for all the ability I still have left. As for others, the only version of awful I know to its absolute core, is the one I have and continue to endure.

Throughout my multiple years of reflection, I have discovered that the grass is RARELY greener on the other side. I have also come to the unfortunate realization, that sometimes just when we think things are at their worst, they get worse. However, regardless of how much worse they get, there is ALWAYS someone who would love to have our bad days. I personally have found that I don't have to search very hard to find that someone, as they are so often our friend, family member, or the unfortunate highlight in our newsfeed. During the days I complained about everything I was no longer able to do, so many others were fighting to take their first or last breath.

During my darkest and deepest moments of desperation, I was simply unable to see that, feel that, or think that way. In addition to all I learned during the darkest days of my diagnosis, I also discovered that by falling victim to this trap, we merely exist... Neither productive to ourselves or anyone else. We inevitably miss out on our own innate ability to inspire, and most importantly, to become inspired.

SPOILER ALERT: The weeks after my last day of tennis in November 2012, turned into months and then years. Although I still hold out hope that one day I may have the chance to play able-bodied tennis again, I'm no longer SIMPLY waiting—waiting as a victim to the incurable, relentless beast living within. The tables turned not because I waited for them to do so, but because I made them.

Although I am not one to say that being diagnosed with MS has in retrospect become a positive thing, because I still think it REALLY sucks, I will say that I have evolved in many ways and have learned many lessons.

Maybe it has something to do with the fact that I'm not overly religious, but whatever the case, I will never say that I was dealt these cards because I was strong enough to handle them. I could never have been strong enough to handle this disaster. Instead, I BECAME strong enough when I simply had no other choice.

I truly believe that before being able to inspire others, it is crucial to first become an inspiration to ourselves. There were multiple days, months and years when I really did not believe my story was worth sharing. For a long time, I saw my journey as one so similar to many: a young woman with MS, fighting to get through each and every day. While this remains true, I eventually came to the realization that this was merely grazing the surface.

There are no two people in this world with the same journey, and this couldn't be any more accurate for those battling MS. This illness has such variety, it's scary. At the end of the day, the only thing two MS patients have exactly the same, is the fact that they've both been diagnosed with

MS. How, when, and why they were diagnosed is a guessing game, just as is the case with their symptoms. While one of them sits in a room full of people, I can almost guarantee you that 99% of the time, no one would be able to accurately pinpoint the person with MS.

Of course when that same person is asked to perform a task like walking, writing, speaking, or recounting past events, it would likely become increasingly obvious. But even still, no two MS patients have the same disease course. I don't know what it's like to lose my vision, just as the person who has lost their vision may not know what it's like to lose their mobility.

I slowly but surely began to realize that my journey was in fact unique, but still wasn't convinced anyone would care much about it. Other than my close family, not many people truly knew the magnitude of suffering I endure on a daily basis, and for a long time, I felt it best to keep it that way. I didn't want to darken anyone's day, or for anyone to feel sorry for me. When I saw friends and family, it was very rarely for an unhappy occasion, and I certainly didn't want to be the one to alter that vibe. Whether I was the host or a guest, I just smiled and said hi, and when asked how I was, I always said "good thanks, and you?"

It wasn't until recently, after time spent writing blogs, that I began to talk about the details of my illness with friends. Yet still, I have never dismissed the fact that when people ask "How are you?" there is a time and a place to say how you REALLY are. When at a large get-together with many people to greet, the last thing I am going to say when asked how I am, is how horrible I actually feel. I've always known that conversations like those are better left for intimate get-togethers at home or at a nearby coffee shop.

Although I knew people truly cared about how I was feeling, I still found it hard to open up completely. I always felt opening up about my journey would be therapeutic, but I just didn't feel face to face was the right way to do it. I knew it would turn into way too much of a monologue, and I never wanted myself or my illness to steal the limelight.

I also knew it would be hard to only tell part of the story, leaving out too many intricate details, so I always kept it to the basics. Now, by writing this book, I can spill the beans in entirety without missing a single one. My intention is certainly not to appear self-centered, but rather to recognize that there are so many other people on a similar journey, and to hope that in some way they will find my story relatable. I want everyone reading this to know that I no longer yearn for greener pastures, as I have come to the blunt realization that often our own problems are the better ones to have.

CHAPTER TEN

My Younger Years

During a recent Athlete Ambassador interview with On-Para (The Ontario Para Network), I was asked about my childhood and how sports have made me a better person. I immediately mentioned my parents and talked about how determined they were to make sure I got involved in athletics at a very young age.

At three years old, my parents got me involved in soccer, which became a competitive sport for me right up until a few years before my MS diagnosis. Soccer required dedication during my adolescent years as we often travelled to tournaments, but it also became my most social sport during adulthood. I always looked forward to it, but it wasn't the sport I was ever most passionate about.

When I was seven years old, I became very competitively involved with figure skating, to the point that I was on the ice six days a week. It was an extremely demanding, difficult and time-consuming sport which required me to be on the ice at six a.m. and again in the late afternoon, to ensure it didn't interfere with my schooling.

Just like soccer, I was able to immerse myself in the sport, thanks to my mom and dad both physically and financially. I have vivid memories of falling more times than not, and always forcing myself to get back up and try again just one more time. I never knew when I would land a jump I had been working on for weeks, but it often felt like an eternity.

As with tennis and every other sport I've played, I LOVED the competition behind figure skating. Nothing was ever recreational for me, and what would have been the purpose of all those early morning practices, if winning wasn't the end goal? My mother dressed me up in all those sparkly outfits, and I always put the pressure on myself to do my best. An intrinsic part of figure skating is making sure, at the very least, you always look the part. Even after missing a jump and feeling nothing but total embarrassment, disappointment, and personal failure, I always got back up with a great big smile on my face.

Until writing this book, I never really realized that figure skating mimics so much of my NEW life in so many ways. Although I definitely yearn for the days when missing a jump was my only problem, I can see how figure skating instilled so many qualities in me, that have served me well in battling my MS.

Whether a literal fall or a hypothetical one, I came to the stern decision that getting back up and trying again was my only option. During my darkest moments of depression, I mastered the art of looking good when feeling terrible, and often continue to smile despite feeling a total loss of control. When my entire body is inflamed with pain, I must go on. I must pull it together, and I must seek the next treatment option.

Just like the days on the ice when I knew it just wasn't my day, I have learned to see things through to the very end.

One bad day of competition or one failed treatment attempt doesn't mean the end of the journey, it just means the end of that chapter.

Figure skating remained a constant part of my life for the next five years, but eventually it became too physically and emotionally demanding, and I decided to transition over to the world of ice hockey, which instantly became my next highly competitive sport. Again, I found myself on the ice, and for a while, the only part of the game I excelled at was skating.

At less than two years old, both my brother Jamie and I were put on skates and fell in love with our newfound abilities. I went in one direction with figure skating, and my brother went in the other direction with hockey. I would attend all of my brother's games and tournaments, and therefore understood all the rules of the game. When I told my parents that I wanted to make the switch from figure skating to hockey, my dad was ecstatic, while my mom was more hesitant. I always had a slim build, and she knew hockey would expose me to the potential for many injuries. But she agreed, and my dad took me to our local sports store and got me all the necessary equipment that same day.

The next step was finding a team. At the time, there were no female teams in hometown Grimsby, so we looked at both the nearby Hamilton and Stoney Creek clubs. While I was always involved in sports in a more competitive way, neither my dad nor I were looking for a house league team, but we knew that may be our only option. However, during our search I was caught by surprise and was offered the chance to play on a competitive team, with girls five years older than me. The team was short in numbers for the season, and since I already knew how to skate, and knew the rules from watching my brother, they figured I would pick up the rest of the game relatively quickly.

Our family was excited and within the next few days my dad registered me in a hockey school. It was definitely a humbling experience, since learning skills like stickhandling and shooting looked so much easier than they really were. But with determination and perseverance, I did learn those skills and became competitive at the sport.

Over the years, I became more and more involved with hockey and played at a relatively high level. Just like with figure skating, I enjoyed the competition most, and always looked forward to the upcoming tournaments. My brother also continued to become more and more involved with hockey, and in time he secured a spot on the Grimsby Peach Kings; our local Junior C team. I continued to go to his games when I wasn't at my own. Needless to say, we were a VERY busy family, but those days played a major role in shaping us into the people we are today.

Getting back to the question asked by OnPara, about what type of impact sports have had on my life... Sports have had a positive impact on my life in many ways. They have taught me so many life lessons and instilled many positive attributes such as self-discipline, determination, and how to follow through on my commitments. They have also taught me how to overcome adversity and how to be both a gracious winner and loser. I have learned through sports, that not every day is a good day, but to always keep pushing and persevering to become the best version of myself. I have learned to set realistic yet challenging goals, and to never give up on their achievement. I have also gained self-confidence and humility and learned how to present myself in a positive way, despite how I may be feeling.

All of these skills have become transferable in almost every aspect of my life, and battling MS is no exception. I thank sports for the grit and tenacity I have developed, and because of these qualities, quitting will never be an option. In my younger years, I never realized how much athletics was teaching me, I just had fun! As a kid, that is what we are supposed to do…but as an adult, it is important to self-reflect on all stages of our life, for every experience is a piece to our own puzzle. By now understanding everything sports have done for me, having my own child involved in sports is not only a given, but also a necessity. I can't wait for him to one day realize, through his own self-reflection, all it has done for him.

BRAVER THAN YOUR BATTLE
Blog Excerpt: "I'm Nothing Without You,"
June 7th 2017

Although I don't remember it, I'm pretty sure I was a big part of the event that occurred on February 26th 1987.

On this very day, my life began…

On this day, I became the daughter to the most amazing parents I could ever ask for.

My parents have always been the type to never miss a soccer game, hockey game, school event, parent-teacher night, graduation, prepping for an interview, or any other special event…and were ALWAYS there for absolutely anything I needed.

There were many years of life that were lived as my previous self, BEFORE disaster struck… and I think knowing how many years were spent playing on competitive soccer and hockey teams, and enjoying many adventures as an active family, is what makes this so heartbreaking for us all.

For people who knew the "old" me, it's often hard for them to look at me the way I am now, and likely wonder what the heck went wrong!?

I can remember many things I used to do, way back until I was seven or eight years old...

But for my parents, they remember every single detail since the day I was born.

They remember the healthy and happy baby, who grew up to be the healthy and happy teenager, who continued on to be the healthy and happy twenty-year-old; remaining active in many sports, and most recently witnessed the love I developed for tennis.

I was on those courts almost every single day playing matches, taking lessons from Joel, and playing tournaments. The initial love that I developed for tennis, was not only for the game itself, but for everything else it brought into my life.

This time of the year is ALWAYS the hardest time for me. The tennis club opens and everyone begins all the outdoor activities they love.

What's even harder, is knowing that there's NOTHING more my parents want, than for me to be out there with them, and I know with 100% certainty that they would trade places with me in a heartbeat if they could. (Which I would never allow...)

Now being a parent to Landon, I feel helpless during the times he simply has a needle or falls and scrapes his chin. As a parent, you always want to be able to protect your child, and not being able to take away their pain is one of the worst feelings a parent will ever experience.

So, when you see your grown daughter suddenly go from running, working full-time, playing sports, and almost always being happy and pain free... to then barely being able to take a few steps and most often confined to a wheelchair, with a level of pain they can't even fathom or fix...

I can't even imagine the magnitude of heartache and pain my parents must feel.

The part that is the most difficult for me is knowing that I am the root cause of their pain. I know it's not REALLY me... I know it's the horrific disease, and there's NOTHING I want more than to be free of this illness, so that they TOO can be free from all the heartache it creates.

Since my diagnosis, my parents have been there for me literally every step of the way. They have researched for me, been with me at my appointments, cried with me, then laughed with me when crying felt like old news, encouraged me, have been patient with me, have loved me unconditionally, and have always been there to lend a helping hand when I struggle to make it up a couple steps.

They have been there giving me massages when I didn't even know where my legs were in space, because the pain was so bad...

They lived every single waking moment during the gut-wrenching sleepless nights, and during my weakest moments, I had to lean on both of them because the strength of one of them alone was not enough to get me into my house.

And the ONE thing I'm pretty positive about, is that they cry behind closed doors because they don't want me to see how much they are hurting.

But Mom and Dad, I know... I know because I am now

a parent. And if Landon were going through something like this, I would be a HOT MESS, for lack of better terms.

I want you to know that I so appreciate the strength you show me, the resilience you instill in me, and persistence you display by always helping me to find the next avenue of attack.

You are the ones who have taught me what strength is all about, because on my worst days when I can't help but break down and have a cry fest, you are only a text, phone call, or five-minute drive away, to pick me right back up and motivate me to keep on fighting the fight.

And as Grandparents... We simply could not ask for better ones. You are the BEST Nonno and Grandma, and we know there is NOTHING that you wouldn't do for us..

If I can end up being half the parent you both have been, I will consider my motherhood journey a success.

I know this whole journey with MS is far from over, but I want you to know how much easier you make it. We are all fighting this thing together and never do I ever feel alone.

I know battling this thing from the side you sit as a parent is not easy by any means. I know It is one of the most difficult things you have ever had to endure. Thank you for being the strength I need when I'm way past the point of weak, and the breath of fresh air you provide when I sometimes feel way beyond suffocated.

There's nothing more I can say other than this...

You are the epitome of "Once a parent ALWAYS a parent."

I love you!

Although I gained a lot of self-confidence through sports, it was off-set by another less favourable aspect of my life. Starting when I was nine years old and continuing through high school, I experienced a great deal of bullying. It was the worst in elementary and middle school, and it's impossible to forget to this day. Although I was never physically attacked, I was verbally bullied to the extent that I didn't want to go to school most mornings. It usually wasn't something specific that was done, but rather a build-up of days of exclusion for no apparent reason.

Being told I couldn't sit at the same table with other kids, or that my clothing wasn't something they would ever wear. It was not being invited to birthday parties or being chosen for gym class teams. It was hurtful and emotionally draining on every level. Girls can be mean, and it can disrupt your entire life. It certainly did for me, and I still don't have any concrete reasons as to why I became a victim.

All of the bullying I endured happened at school and never on any sports teams. At the time, I wasn't able to understand that. Obviously my teammates didn't find me a bad person, so why were those girls at school so ruthless? Although it infuriated my mother, it was hard to do anything about it. Conversations were had with the mothers of the bullying girls, as well as our teachers, but it did nothing except make the bullying worse.

Due to the nature of the bullying, there was nothing in particular that could be stopped. As I mentioned, it wasn't WHAT they were doing, nearly as much as what they WEREN'T doing. A casual bystander would probably not even have known that the bullying was such an issue. The girls should have won an academy award for their acting skills, whenever they were confronted by a teacher or a parent. I can still remember their fake smiles so clearly. I truly believe they took my shyness and kindness for weakness. They saw me as the perfect person to target, and they did so in the most typical form of bullying. They remained under the radar, until one day I had had enough and told them all off.

I was sick and tired of trying to fit into a group that I was better off without. In middle school and high school, it remained an issue, yet this time I had less patience for it. The one problem with a small town, is that almost everyone knows everyone else. So when our middle schools merged into the only public high school in town, the bullies developed their little cult of people who just decided I was someone they didn't want around. I also ended up telling all of them off too, and it couldn't have felt more empowering!

Needless to say, I never grew up with a close group of girlfriends who then became lifelong friends. I tried to have this, but it just wasn't in my cards. Instead, I developed individual friends through different aspects and times in my life who I can genuinely say are TRUE friends. Around them, I don't have to try to be accepted. Even now in a wheelchair, I can honestly say I have better friends than ever before. The ones who didn't want to deal with my new situation were released like free birdies, and the ones who I can truly rely on, and the ones who sincerely care about my well-being, remain a constant support in all aspects of my life.

Now, more than ever, I am less concerned about having a tribe of friends, and way more concerned about growing and nurturing the genuine friendships I do have. I consider myself so fortunate to be surrounded by people who are truly interested in seeing me flourish and succeed, and I am grateful to have found many of these new friends during the most difficult part of my life thus far. I learned that having a group of girlfriends is SO overrated and if anything, it can be more exhausting to ensure everyone is always happy.

I eventually learned my own worth, and although my self-confidence was absolutely shattered during my school-age years, I found a way to rebuild it through sports and continued to put the pieces back together during my four years spent at Brock University, as well as the almost six years I spent working in the sales industry. It certainly was not easy to gain back something so fragile. I knew at any moment it could be shattered again, but self-confidence is absolutely a vital part of any person's life, and I desperately wanted it back in mine. I wanted to be happy again.

The first part in gaining some of my confidence back, was living independently on campus during my first year at Brock. I was able to meet new friends, and since I was living in a residence, it was hard to avoid people. There was always someone around to chat with, even if it was just about the weather. I never became close friends with those I met in my first year, but at least I met people. My parents only lived twenty-five minutes from the campus, so I could have easily stayed home and saved a LOT of money, but I wanted the university "experience," as I knew it would serve me well.

For the remaining three years of my time at Brock, I lived off campus with roommates and got to experience the veteran side of student life. My roommates and I were forced to become more responsible in a variety of ways. We had to ensure that bills were paid, groceries were bought, the garbage put out, and the house cleaned—all on top of studying for exams and getting assignments completed. I gained a lot of my confidence back during these later years as a student, as I became closer friends with my roommates and it really became obvious that I hadn't been the problem back in my adolescent years, it was THEM.

I also found the time to play on a competitive hockey team during my third and fourth years, and I came to understand many things about myself. Not only did I realize that there were many people both in university and through athletics who saw the good in who I was, but I started to believe in myself again. I started to acknowledge how well I did in class, how responsible, committed, and trustworthy I was, and really started to have faith in the valuable employee I'd soon become. The pieces were slowly but surely mending back together.

Graduating from Brock University in 2009 with an Honours Degree in Sport Management, was certainly a proud moment that paved the way for the next six years of my life. Almost immediately after graduating, I began my career as an Employee Benefits Specialist. I touched on this in an earlier chapter, but I want to touch on it again, as it really was a turning point for me in regaining my self-confidence. Although I had many in-office responsibilities, at the end of the day, it was first and foremost a sales job.

I was expected to build new relationships and nurture existing ones, with both Financial Advisors and their group benefit clients, who in turn became our clients. As previously mentioned, in this role I was considered the "middle man" and therefore was required to make sure both the Advisor and their clients remained happy enough to continue doing business with us. I had sales targets which I was always aiming to reach, but it was far from easy. I was required to travel in a relatively large territory and attend meetings with either solely the Financial Advisor, or both the Advisor and client, and was also required to perform training sessions at different London Life offices.

Due to the nature of the job, I had to appear and act confident for many different reasons. I wanted my clients to trust in my abilities, and that had to start with feeling confident myself. I had to go into a meeting ready to answer a variety of questions, and equipped to offer them unique and appealing solutions. It was my job to solve problems in a confident yet genuine manner.

With my time spent at Great-West Life eventually leading me into my own role as a Financial Advisor, I had to be more confident than ever before. Everything was now mine to gain or to lose, and no one was going to do it for me. I had to make cold calls, develop plans, enter into business agreements, and became responsible for aspects of both businesses and individuals. Without regaining confidence in my prior role, I would not have had the success I did in my first and only year as a London Life Financial Advisor.

By the end of my first year, my health deteriorated and I had to go on disability leave AGAIN. I thought I would eventually be able to go back to work, but I was so very wrong. At the time I was forced to stop working, it had been about a year after my last day playing tennis. I went from walking with a limp, to barely being able to make it into meetings using a cane. I tried with everything I had to continue attending meetings, but it simply became far too difficult, and practically impossible. Not only was it not safe for me to drive on most days, but I physically was not able to get into client's businesses or homes without an immense struggle.

The job itself was extremely stressful, with income being one hundred percent commission and therefore never knowing when I would make my next dollar. Although I tried to remain confident as I BARELY made my way into meetings, the inevitable was just around the corner.

I knew I had to stop months before I actually did. I always held out a tiny bit of hope that one day I'd wake up and things would be better, but I knew the reality of the situation all too well. Just as rapidly as I declined physically, my self-confidence which I had worked SO hard to rebuild, plummeted. I felt myself hitting rock-bottom and I felt so useless. I didn't know how to react and I felt more like a victim than ever before. I had never experienced the feeling of being unable to solve my own problems until then.

I kept thinking there must be a way out of this chaos... this disaster called my life. I imagined days like this may happen eventually, but I wished with everything I had, that it would never come to this. I so badly wanted to find the answers to how I would make it through the next forty or fifty years of my life, being so disabled, weak, depressed and in pain. But more than all that, I needed to find ways to muster up the strength, perseverance and determination to make it happen.

As it became increasingly clear that 'getting up' physically would continue to be a challenge, I knew I had to begin the process of strengthening my mind. I had to make the decision that MS was not going to win and that I would find a way out of this mess. At that point, I didn't have a clue as to how I would make this happen, but I simply knew it had to be done.

CHAPTER ELEVEN

Grieving The Loss Of Myself

ACCEPTANCE ISN'T SURRENDERING

Throughout the years leading up to today, I have had many more moments that shattered those broken pieces of self-confidence into mere remnants, yet also other moments when the pieces slowly started to mend back together again, and this time in a far different way.

I continued to wonder why I couldn't just "snap out of it" so to speak. I had come to accept my diagnosis, and had even accepted the fact that my mobility had been severely affected. I certainly was aware of the cards I'd been dealt, so what was my problem? Why couldn't I just move on?

I continuously fathomed the possible answers to this question, but each and every day I found myself in a new battle, against the same opponent. I simply COULDN'T move on. The mental struggle was becoming just as debilitating as my physical symptoms, and I knew that the first step in building mental resilience was putting this unknown to rest. I was always a problem solver, whether at school or at work, but I had never been faced with a personal problem of this magnitude to solve.

The worst I had ever had to experience was the bullying or a romantic relationship gone wrong. But the more my world was turned upside down by my new diagnosis, the more those other problems took a back seat. While recognizing every part of my life is part of my story, and has played a part in shaping who I am today, I had never had to face anything this severe. No matter how real or personally disruptive past problems were, the main difference was that they could be solved.

They were times in my life which most definitely left an impact, but ones I can look back on now and be happy they ended. That's the main difference between a chronic illness and most problems in life: as long as you are still living, it simply NEVER ends. The pain, fatigue, impairment of mobility, heartache, grief, all of it… It never EVER ends.

In that moment of harsh reality being slammed in my face, I gained clarity. I had already done the hard work of reaching the point of acceptance, and I now finally knew what I had to do to move on: I needed to grieve the loss of myself.

At first it felt a little strange to be having these thoughts, since I had believed grief was only a process to go through after someone passed away. I guess I just did not have enough life experience to understand that the process of grief was necessary in a variety of scenarios. It became increasingly obvious that it was necessary in my situation, when I constantly caught myself crying over the things I would never be able to do again, and the different aspects of my life that would be forever changed. It simply made sense that I had felt a funeral for my old self was more than necessary. Just like with grief when we lose someone, I knew it wasn't going to be an overnight thing, but rather a process that may quite possibly never end.

The main difference between grieving the loss of ourselves versus someone else, is that we aren't dead! We are still here and very much remember all the times we were once able to do something which we no longer can, and have vivid memories of the life we once complained about for other reasons, yet one that now appears so incredibly perfect.

Although we may now realize and accept the fact that we are no longer the person we once were, we also still must hold out hope for the day we regain even a sliver of who we once were, and the life we once had. Although we accept the fact that we now must rely on not only a wheelchair, cane or walker, but are also dependent on others, we still must strive for the day when we regain partial or complete independence.

Throughout the process of grieving the loss of myself, I have been forced to find new ways of being independent and thus new ways of being happy. Through finding ways of regaining independence, I can say with complete certainty that even in a wheelchair, I have regained confidence. For me and my journey, the key to all of this, is playing the lead role in my own story and making it all happen.

I've learned that if we always wait for things to magically mend themselves on their own and return to their prior state, we will wait our entire lives. As living beings, our life is constantly changing, and so must we. We MUST NOT expect things to remain in perfect balance and we MUST react to the cards we are dealt. If we merely wait, we will most definitely be left in the dust of our own happiness. So, get uncomfortable and make the change you know you need. At the very least, take the first step and become witness to the greatness you will find with every step thereafter. It's not a race, but even the slowest participant must start.

During my darkest days, when depression was at an all-time high, I just could not see how I would ever be able to be happy again. I didn't try to make things happen, and at that point, I had mentally given up. It was the worst combination of my own thoughts, unknowns about my future, and my own indecisiveness regarding what I should do next. I didn't give myself the gift of looking beyond my new disability and finding other ways to do things.

When I let go of the person I once was, I really started LIVING as a person with MS. I realized that no one could do it for me, and putting an end to all the self-pity was crucial. I needed to stop asking the question "why me?" because no matter how many times I asked, and to how many different people, I came to the same two conclusions: 1) No one knows and 2) it's STILL you.

When I really took the time to analyze that newfound information, I started to see things in a different light. I began to realize that all I was doing was wasting time and wasting my life. Don't get me wrong—there are still days and still times when I am more emotional than others, and these thoughts enter my mind, but instead of it being a daily occurrence, it is much less often.

I know that I deserve the right to have a day when things are just super ridiculously difficult, and I want nothing more than to cry and let it all out… and I have decided this is perfectly reasonable. I have gained enough clarity to know that those moments are not going to drastically change anything, but for those short-lived moments, I don't care. The buildup of stress and frustration needs a release, and sometimes, just sometimes, having a temper tantrum is the best way.

I don't see this as a regression in the positive progression I have made in my life over the years. I simply see it as a necessity to continue being the best version of myself. Everyone needs an outlet, and this is even more true for someone who has completely or partially lost the person they once were. Loss is loss regardless of the reason, and we need to heal in a way that is most suitable to our personal situation. In a scenario like mine, when grieving the loss of ourselves is necessary, it is an on-going process and it will continuously change as our illness and/or lives change.

I don't believe grief ever comes to an end. Of course, its path leads in different directions for everyone, but if I have come to one conclusion regarding grief in my personal journey, it's that grieving the loss of myself is not only beneficial, it is crucial. If it wasn't for allowing myself to take the time to let go of certain phases of my life and to welcome new ones I wish never existed, I wouldn't be able to wake up every morning with a purpose and play a productive role in society.

For so long I felt that ship had sailed—the one where I was anywhere close to a productive citizen of society. There were days I truly could not figure out what my new purpose was, as I sat on the couch day in and day out, in pain and misery. But once I decided I could make new purposes for myself, life started to seem even the slightest bit more optimistic. In the earliest phases of this personal transformation, I didn't fully understand what these new purposes would entail, but I found comfort in at least knowing they could exist.

I set the goal of playing wheelchair tennis in five years if

I wasn't able to return to able-bodied tennis, and Joel and I thought more seriously about having a child. Although we spent two years debating this topic and had varying opinions, I never wavered from my maternal instincts and my deep intuition, that becoming a mother would be one of the best things to ever happen to me. I knew it would be difficult, but I also knew it would instantly become one of my ultimate purposes as my "new" self.

Although I genuinely knew that becoming a mother would test our relationship in many ways, I definitely didn't put nearly enough thought into how troublesome the pregnancy would be on my body. To be honest, by only five weeks I actually had dark wandering thoughts about if I had made a mistake, and if I would even make it out of the pregnancy alive. Being hit with all the difficulties of my diagnosis in general, I had built levels of resilience I never thought possible and I therefore became less and less dramatic about the less important things in life. I became better at solving daily problems that would await me from the moment I opened my eyes each morning.

In large part, this is what made my thoughts about my pregnancy so real and scary. I became someone who was forced to find a way through even the most challenging situations, yet I simply couldn't see my way through this one. Rapidly, my pregnancy became the absolute most difficult aspect of my journey thus far, and little did I know, it was only the beginning.

CHAPTER TWELVE

Oh, Baby

(SUMMER 2014)

I knew I was pregnant. We BOTH knew.

We went out for dinner at Brasas in Niagara Falls, and had to leave soon after we were seated. The nausea was out of control. Every single type of meat that was offered seemed like the most unappetizing thing I had ever seen. I kept trying to talk myself out of the overwhelming smells and the internal summersaults that had rapidly taken control of my tummy, but it was a no-go. Nothing was stopping the inevitable. So, we paid and we left. Yes, an $80 dinner down the drain...LITERALLY.

Joel was a real trooper. He never even complained that all he had to eat from that $80 dinner, were three bites of quinoa salad. Right away he said "You're pregnant!" But I was not quite so sure. I thought it was probably just the flu, trying not to get my hopes up. However, in my mind, all fingers and toes were crossed.

Over the next couple of days I started to feel menstrual-like cramps, and of course I did my due diligence with repetitive Google searches. From what I found on the web, menstrual cramps COULD be early signs of pregnancy, OR they could just be the usual warning sign that your little friend is on the way. The few days I had to wait before taking a pregnancy test felt like weeks. I had to wait until the day of or day after my expected period, before I could put my curiosity to rest. I was warned that taking a test so early could give false results, but I couldn't wait any longer—I had to know.

Finally, a week after that disastrous dinner at Brasas, Joel's early prediction was confirmed. Baby Cruz was on the way! The morning I took the test, I caught Joel just before he headed out the door and broke him the life-changing news. We were both over the moon with emotion, yet neither of us came up with many words in the moment. He had to go to work, and we both continued on with our day as usual.

Although in retrospect it may have been better to have saved the surprise for the evening, when we would have been able to react together, I knew I wouldn't have been able to hold in the news for the entire day. At least this way, we had all day long to ponder what our new lives may entail. It didn't happen right away, but over the course of the day, it sunk in that I was going to be a mother, despite all the obstacles that were stacked in front of us, sky-high.

Unfortunately, that feeling of expected bliss quickly got squashed by a number of variables totally out of our control. The first one being no more meds. Zilch, Nada, NOTHING. I understood I would no longer be able to take any medication which I was on to control my MS symptoms, but I never thought about the drug I was on to stabilize my insomnia. I actually did think of it at one point long before I got pregnant, but my doctor misinformed me that the best plan of action was to continue taking the medication until I was indeed pregnant. This ended up being the absolute WORST piece of advice I have ever received from a certified physician. There is no way I would have gotten pregnant until I had properly weaned myself off of it, if I had known everything I would face. No one in their right mind would sign themselves up for what I endured. Something I still, to this day, consider nothing less than unintentional self-inflicted TORTURE.

I never knew what "rebound insomnia" was, until I went seven nights (168 hours) without even one MINUTE of sleep. No exaggeration. It was so bad, that at times I felt that it was never going to get better, and that I was NEVER going to sleep again… that I may not even make it out alive.

As the sleepless nights went on, I was going absolutely insane. I was trying every bed in our house like the three bears, and when that didn't work, I tried sleeping in every bed at my parent's house. My mom would spend most hours awake with me rubbing my legs, my back and doing anything else that would give me even the slightest bit of relief. Once a mother always a mother!

The nights were long and the days even longer. Every single minute that passed was consumed with the thought and fear of having to try to sleep again the next night. I was so sleep deprived, I didn't even know where I was half of the time and I had no idea where my body was in space. I could feel nothing but the most excruciating pain ever imaginable. No matter the level of physical exhaustion, my mind would not turn off.

I kept imagining how all of this would be downright torturous for anyone without a chronic illness… but what ramped this up five thousand notches is that I DO have a chronic illness, and even losing a few hours of sleep is disastrous for many MS patients. I remember before I was pregnant, when for whatever reason I was unable to sleep, and thinking how awful it was going to be the next day. I remember thinking how difficult it would be to get through the minutes of every passing hour and how much worse my pain would become.

As the nights ticked on by without a single second of sleep, I wondered how it was even legal to allow someone to go through such mental and physical agony, without there being some sort of option to subside even one-eighth of the torture. I then quickly remembered that anyone else having to go through 168 hours of no sleep, most likely wouldn't have MS.

No matter how bad things got, there was nothing anybody could do, and at only four weeks pregnant I had NO idea how I was going to make it through thirty-six more, nor what shape I'd be in at the end. There are still no words to describe the level of pain my body was under, and it got worse with every sleepless minute. On a good day my body feels like it weighs 500 pounds, but after seven nights of no sleep, there were parts of me that were literally paralyzed.

What made things even more difficult was knowing I had pills right beside my bed which I knew would allow me to sleep. However, I also knew how bad they were for our unborn child, and knowing this fact was more than enough to never allow myself to take a single one. It didn't matter how bad I got, or how many sleepless nights I had to endure, there was NO way I was taking one of those pills. Only four weeks into my pregnancy, I learned what it truly meant to make sacrifices as a mother. I TRULY got to know what "For the Love of a Child" REALLY meant.

Eventually I did start sleeping but in VERY small increments and I never exceeded four hours a night my entire pregnancy. I would hear other pregnant women talk about how quickly time was FLYING by and how they couldn't wait to no longer have all the back pain.

Of course, it was difficult to hear those comments, when my body literally felt like it was being ripped apart in multiple directions. But what was I going to say? "I would love to ONLY have your back pain?" Although I thought it, I made sure I kept that thought to myself, because no matter how awful I felt, I also realized that from their perspective, they felt awful too. And there was no level of explanation that would make them understand how my body felt. No matter what I thought or how I felt, I just smiled and agreed that the back pain was BRUTAL. Remember...the only level of awful we know is the one we have experienced.

Without a doubt, the severe insomnia was by far the worst part of my pregnancy. Due to the insomnia and my constant level of pain, in combination with the god-awful morning sickness, I ended up losing twenty-five pounds in my first two trimesters. With only weighing 130 pounds to start, losing twenty-five pounds was a BIG deal. My usual weight is around 115 pounds, and the only reason I had gained the extra fifteen pounds before getting pregnant, was because of the prednisone I had just finished taking for a recent MS flare up.

For a long, long time, the only thing I could eat were crackers. In my third trimester, I was able to force myself to eat enough that I gained fifteen pounds back. I was constantly worried that all the stress from sleepless nights, combined with my inability to eat, was harming our baby. I was already blaming myself for not being the best mom, and this definitely took a toll on my mental state. I was already highly irritable from lack of sleep and hormone swings, and this was just icing on the cake.

Although I was ensured by my OB that babies take what they need from their mother, I still had a really tough time dealing with the inability to be better. But as the weeks passed and I found myself into the latter half of my second trimester, I saw and felt for myself that Landon was perfectly fine. Not only did an ultrasound confirm his "ahead of the game" size and weight, I also felt those powerful kicks and rock-hard jabs. Turns out my boy had his mama's back from the get-go!

Day by day, week by week, time continued to pass slower than molasses, and at thirty-five weeks I told my OB that I needed my baby out of me ASAP. I needed to get back on treatment, and more than anything, I needed to SLEEP.

The earliest he agreed to induce me was 38.5 weeks, and that happened to fall on New Year's day. The other catch was that he was going to be on vacation, and I would therefore have a different OB for delivery... but I was desperate, and none of those glitches were enough to alter my decision. Just like that, I was scheduled to be induced at The West Lincoln Memorial Hospital in Grimsby, Ontario, on New Year's Day, 2015.

I didn't sleep much the night before (shocking, I know), and I started the day with a range of emotions at an all-time high. No matter how horrible I felt physically, I couldn't help but feel an overwhelming sense of excitement. In just a matter of hours, everything we had overcome, endured, and battled would all be worth it.

As it happened, I never had to be induced, as I ended up going into labour naturally just hours after arriving at the hospital. It was a long and intense labour—eighteen hours and forty-three minutes to be exact. My plan was always to have a natural labour, without an epidural or any other pain medication, and that is what I had.

I think wanting a natural labour came from a place of truly believing I could do it, and that it would be better for Landon and me in the long run. First of all, I knew that la-bour pain would eventually come to an end, something I was never able to say for MS pain. I also had been warned that the numbing effects of an epidural could potentially affect more of the body than what is intended, and that was a risk I was not willing to take. Furthermore, having an epidural would heighten my risk for a C-section, which was also something I wanted to avoid if at all possible.

Fast forward to the final four hours of my labour, when I asked Joel how crazy I was for turning down the epidural, with my contractions less than thirty seconds apart. Never did I EVER imagine how painful they would be.

But after 38.5 weeks of torturous mayhem, I knew at this point it was truly down to mind over matter. Regardless of the intensity, I continued to remind myself that labour pain was only temporary. The comfort of knowing I had already gotten through one hundred percent of my toughest days, allowed me to literally PUSH past the finish line.

On Jan 2nd at 4:43 a.m., weighing seven pounds even, baby Landon Fernando Cruz was FINALLY here. And al-though I was in awe and utter amazement of the most ador-able little being that lay on my chest, my very first words were "Thank God it's over!"

CHAPTER THIRTEEN

The Mother I've Become

Let's just cut right to the chase…being a mother is HARD! No matter who you are, what you're facing, where you've come from, where you're headed, what you've overcome or what you're still battling, being a mother is downright difficult.

Yes, it is rewarding, but it is by far one of the most challenging journeys in life. We mothers like to relate to other mothers by knowing that everything we are going through, and all the obstacles we face, are shared by millions of other mothers who are going through the "same thing." The thing is, just like MS, no two children and therefore no two motherhood journeys are the same. Although the one common thread about being a mother is raising a child, it is my personal belief that all these other things we encounter while doing so are merely similar, and not so much the same at all.

From the baby who won't sleep, to the one who won't stop crying, to the high-pitched teething screams, to the formula fed baby, or the baby still being nursed… To the toddlers who only say "no," to the ones who babble all day… From the children who are being bullied to the ones bullying others, and from the teenager struggling in school, to the ones who question every single rule…

ALL of what we may or may not face while navigating our way through motherhood is only similar, because no two mothers nor two children are the same. From the sleepless nights to the potty training days, to the stubborn teenage years and everything in-between…OF COURSE all these stages are relatable from one mother to another. (*as a side note, please realize I am only using "mother" versus father or parent simply because I am a mother, and I am making references from this point of view.*)

Although there are similarities, what remains very different in every mother's journey is the personal story each of us hold. That is everything we must battle, overcome or modify in order to accomplish any one of the "motherly" tasks with which we are faced.

For the longest time, WAY before I was a mother, I had a vision in my mind of being the "perfect" mother to the "perfect" child and doing everything the same way every other mother did. (As if I truly knew what that way was.)

I had imagined the sleepless nights, the nursing, the teething stages, and even the days I would keep my baby attached to me in one of those carriers, just to get something done. I had envisioned picking him or her up and carrying them on my hip, taking long walks on nice days, and frantically running to the car while getting caught in the rain. I had envisioned going everywhere and anywhere I wanted with my baby, and carrying multiple bags plus a car seat all at once.

I had envisioned teaching my son or daughter how to play every sport I knew, taking them to the park, to play dates, to the mall, to the doctor all on my OWN, and doing everything else a "normal" mother would do. That WAS my vision, but of course that was all before MS.

My vision of being a mother changed drastically not only after my diagnosis, but after living this life with a long list of debilitating symptoms in tow... Symptoms previously discussed, that included overwhelming physical fatigue combined with severe nerve pain and the inability to walk more than a couple of steps... and only having one hand free while taking those steps, because the other was holding onto whatever was beside me for dear life.

Although what I had envisioned had started to change, it wasn't until after Landon was born that reality really hit, and I was forced to face the fact that I WASN'T going to be the mother I had envisioned all those years before. That being said, nothing was going to stop me from being the best mother I could be, as I always knew I would give it all I had.

Regardless of being forced to do things differently than I had once thought, it has taken a very long time to mentally get to the point where I'm at now—that is accepting the fact that I am the mother I've BECOME and not the mother I THOUGHT I'd be.

I've embraced many aspects of the mother I've become. In the first few years of Landon's life, I wasn't the mother who could get there in time for most falls. I wasn't the mother who could EVER afford to worry about the things that dropped on the floor, and then went directly into his mouth. I AM the mother who has bribed my child, just to make him cooperate when I've reached my breaking point.

I have NEVER been the mother who nursed, or the one who got up in the middle of the night to get Landon a bottle. (Joel took on that challenge.) I was NEVER the mother to go on long walks, carry him on my hip, or carry multiple bags and a car seat all at once. I was NEVER able to play with Landon in our front yard, driveway, splash pad, or any other open space when he was younger, for fear of him wandering off and not being able to protect him from busy streets, or any other danger.

But there are the things I HAVE done and continue to do, although at a much more modified pace and in a very different way. I remember the times I took Landon to the mall, took him to the doctor and even on a mother-son lunch date. I did go for walks, only to the stop sign and back, and on REALLY good days maybe a street further... but never have I gone anywhere, or done any of these things without immense fatigue, pain, and difficulty to the point that I was gripping the stroller with every ounce of energy I had left, JUST to remain upright.

That being said, regardless of the way I've done things, how much or how little I've done things, or at what modified pace, I've done them, and for that I am so incredibly proud. I am also extremely grateful for my parents, who have been a part of Landon's life since the day he was born, helping me in ways for which I will always be grateful. They are an endless line of support for us both, easing the difficulties at birth, and they have continued to do so in every way they can—the absolute BEST parents and grandparents.

Through all of the challenges and triumphs, one of my biggest hopes for Landon, is for him to one day see all the things in this life he can accomplish through problem solving, thinking outside the box, getting creative, pushing himself out of his comfort zone, and realizing there is never a challenge too big or a problem not worth solving. The moment we decide to make it happen, we begin to figure out HOW to make it happen. The key is wanting it badly enough.

With Landon now five years old and in his first year of kindergarten, I could not be prouder of the little man he's becoming. Due to everything I can't do, he has been forced to help me in ways he may never even realize. He has become sensitive to my pain, intuitive about my limitations, and always there to give me a kiss during one of my biggest meltdowns.

I am FAR from the "normal" mother I thought I'd be—but then again, what's normal? No mother has it easy, and we are all fighting battles most of us know nothing about.

We post pictures of ourselves and our families in the perfect setting, with the perfect smiles and the perfect tagline…but behind the façade, there is almost ALWAYS a story which only we and our best supporters know. A story that pushes us out of our momentary bliss and back into the reality we face every single day.

If there is one thing MS has made me thankful for, it's the resilience it has instilled in me as a person and a mother. I will NOT quit because quitting is simply not an option. No matter how hard it may get, Landon will ALWAYS be my personal cheerleader and everlasting motivation as he chants "GO Mommy GO!"

CHAPTER FOURTEEN

The Girl In The Wheelchair

(2017-PRESENT)

Ever since that dreadful day on the courts in November 2012, when I officially lost the vast majority of my mobility, I have kept pushing. I thought if I just kept moving, my brain would wake up and everything would go back to normal. This way of thinking continued for a long while, as I pushed through my pregnancy and the first few years of Landon's life, with a cane as a mobility aid, but one that wasn't nearly stable enough.

My independence and confidence as a person and as a mother diminished steadily, when I had to turn down invitations to go out, and when I did go out someplace, I had to hobble in with the assistance of two people. Yeah, imagine that visual: dressed up and confident while sitting in front of the mirror, and it all vanishes the moment you try to stand up and simply can't—or you can, but with the help of an arm on each side, and then you freeze. The time comes to move your feet, and no matter how badly you want them to move, they just won't listen. Eventually they start to shuffle in some odd, spastic way, and everyone in the entire room turns around to stare at you…Yeah, not the best feeling.

Granted, those people could be thinking a variety of things, but I wager that a vast majority felt pity—the one thing I NEVER want people to feel for me. So, as I hobble around with the aid of two people, feeling the fatigue and pain kick it up a notch with each and every step, I stand as tall as I can and give the most beaming smile possible. I would then get multiple "You look GREAT Gillian!" compliments, and I believed them. I was thankful for those compliments, but the problem was I didn't FEEL great. I felt deflated both physically and emotionally every single time, and enough was enough.

It was too many invitations declined, awkward entries into a crowd, and the inability to do everything I could possibly do for Landon, when I knew the traditional form of mobility was no longer functional—it was time to find a new way. It was time to face the next inevitable aspect of my future: THE WHEELCHAIR.

From the blank stares, to the worried stares, to the curious stares, to the "I remember you" stares, to the "I'm pretending not to look" stares, and to the quick glances that really aren't that quick… It is human nature and will never change. The moment you transition from walking to wheeling, it instantly becomes your harsh new reality.

Since the very first moments of my MS diagnosis, the thought of life in a wheelchair instantly entered my mind, but as I mentioned before, it was a potential reality I DREADED. I simply couldn't fathom how THAT type of life could be filled with happiness or success. Always being an athlete, with sports an integral part of my being, I just could not see how life would or could go on in a wheelchair. I literally saw it as the absolute worst-case scenario, and never imagined my mind could change. Why would it? In the beginning, despite my diagnosis, I was still fully able-bodied and still fully able to do everything I wanted, the WAY I wanted. However, only two years post diagnosis when my mobility dwindled away, so did my zest for life—my smile, laughter, and positive outlook on my future slipped away, too.

Each day I fought SO hard to take microscopic steps, and instead of celebrating a win on the court, I began celebrating the days I was able to walk to the bathroom, cook a meal, stand for a mere thirty seconds, successfully step off of a curb, or complete any other task I once took for granted.

Only two years post diagnosis, the person I was became the person I never thought I'd be. My ability to drive and work quickly became luxuries I used to have, and were additional pieces of my independence that quickly vanished.

I spent day after day crying more hours than not, and each and every day was filled with nerve pain, chronic fatigue, and the unknowns of my future. My ability to contribute to my family became smaller and smaller, and my purpose in life became almost nonexistent.

Just when I thought things couldn't get any worse, life proved me wrong and my worst-case scenario became my harsh reality. The energy exerted to take two simple steps was no longer functional and this girl became "The Girl in the Wheelchair."

You may be wondering why I refer to myself that way, and the simple answer is that I have learned how to OWN it. Yup, it was a turn of events I never saw coming. Wouldn't you think my worst-case scenario coming to fruition would launch me further into a life of misery? YA, me too... but it didn't!

The moment I became a daily wheelchair user was the moment I regained my independence. I no longer had to rely on an arm to hold or a wall to grab. I no longer had to avoid going places I so desperately wanted to go, and best of all, I no longer had to play victim to my illness. Living in a wheelchair started to highlight all the things I was now ABLE to do, and it triggered my persistent pursuit of becoming an athlete once again.

I will dive deeper into this in the next chapter, but for now, you must know this: Weelchair Tennis has changed my life. I know, it's a pretty bold statement to make about a sport right? But it's the truth. Wheelchair Tennis opened my eyes to all I could be despite my illness, and all the aspects of my life I could regain including my independence, confidence and overall happiness. My first time being back on the court rather than on the sidelines, was a surreal and empowering moment.

Through the use of a chair, I developed the ability to see the world through a different lens, and started practicing gratitude on a regular basis. I started to live each day with my life-changing affirmation as guidance and a daily reminder of all the things I have gained rather than lost:

"There's ALWAYS someone who would love to have your bad days."

No phrase has ever resonated with me more deeply. Although my situation presents a multitude of challenges, I know there are SO many people who have it worse and would trade places with me in an instant. During this time of self-reflection, I began to realize that a wheelchair isn't disabling at all. I not only learned how to survive in it, I learned how to THRIVE in it.

Of course living life in a chair is far from ideal, but it

is also far from the "worst-case scenario" I had pinned in my mind. I'm still fully aware of all the different types of looks I get, but I no longer see this in a negative light. I can once again enter a room with confidence, knowing that a wheelchair is merely a mode of transportation and one I am grateful to have. I know that people will often wonder what happened, and it will always be my story to tell.

I know that no matter what I do, I will always stand out in a crowd, and this is a fact I have learned to embrace. Whether I'm remembered from an interesting conversation, a sparkly accessory, or as the girl in the wheelchair, it's neither here nor there, because true confidence comes from within.

Do I still have dark days? ABSOLUTELY, and I know I always will. I have days I still wonder why. I have days I still break down and cry, and I have days I still dream about the person I once was. No day is easy, and often the pain is unbearable to the point no words can accurately describe it. I have many days I don't know how I am going to do it, and EVERY day I wish I could do more. I have MULTIPLE reasons why this isn't fair and MULTIPLE symptoms I can't ignore.

However, through all of this, I have learned that regardless of the battles we face, it is the overcoming of these battles that strengthens us, shapes us, and prepares us for the mental resilience needed to succeed in this life. It's through all the adversity overcome, battles won, and grieving the loss of myself, that I have learned one simple yet crucial life lesson: No matter how difficult, how painful, how exhausting, or how emotionally draining it may be, OWNING our OWN reality is what it's all about.

CHAPTER FIFTEEN

An Altered Life, An Altered Mindset

(APRIL 2018)

Now before I get too far into how being a daily wheelchair user has changed my life, I want to put to rest one simple misconception that many people have about MS and exercise, leading to why a wheelchair is often unavoidable. I won't talk about this for long, but this simple message needs to be understood by anyone trying to understand MS—so here it is: MS IS A NEUROLOGICAL CONDITION.

What does this mean in relation to muscle strengthening or exercise? It simply means that some of us (including myself) just aren't physically able to do enough repetitions of an exercise in order for it to be functional and provide results. Why?

Due to this beautiful thing called MS, my own immune system attacks my central nervous system—the system responsible for every single move we make and thought we have. More specifically, it attacks the myelin sheath, which is the coating around every single nerve we have. When my immune system decides to attack my central nervous system, it leaves damage along the myelin sheath, which is responsible for message transmission between the brain and every other part of the body.

Think of it as similar to the coating on the outside of a wire or cable, and a mouse decides to come along and have a nibble, leaving the cord with holes along the way. The cord may still work to a certain degree, but it won't transmit information as quickly or as accurately as it did, pre-mouse nibbles.

THAT is exactly what happens with MS. I have a massive lesion between my shoulder blades, which doesn't allow messages to get from my brain, through my spinal cord and to every muscle below my chest, at the proper speed and in the proper form. THIS is what leads to all the debilitating symptoms I've mentioned in previous chapters, and this is why my MS-affected muscles are unable to simply "GET STRONGER." To put it a different way, If I am trying to strengthen my hamstring, but that muscle only receives minimal nerve supply, it doesn't matter how badly I want it to react and strengthen—the message isn't getting through, and all I am doing is causing more unnecessary pain and fatigue= Not functional.

It wasn't easy getting to this realization myself, but once I did, it was about finding other ways to be mobile. The transformation then started happening both mentally and physically, and I not only became "The Girl in the Wheelchair," but I started to transition into the best version of myself I have ever been.

My Life-Changing Statement

"If I can't play able-bodied tennis in five years, I'll play wheelchair tennis." I spoke these exact words in 2013, a year after that night in November 2012, when tennis as I knew it was over. I had thought these words before the day I said them out loud, but I had kept them a secret, hoping that they wouldn't need to come to fruition. I had hoped so badly that I would play able-bodied tennis again, but I was fed up. I was fed up with leaving my ability to play tennis again to chance... to the "maybe."

I was never one to just leave anything I wanted badly enough to chance, and tennis was no different. It had become my biggest passion and social activity. I knew I had to play again, and just like coming to the realization that I needed a different mode of transportation in this life, I came to the same realization regarding tennis. If I couldn't be an able-bodied athlete, I'd become a para athlete.

I was sure of this, so sure that I felt it necessary to say these words out loud, in my living room, with Joel and my mother as witnesses. It was still five years out, and just as I did, they held out hope that I would return to the able-bodied game, but were happy I had a back-up plan.

Even though the plan was formulated for a date so far in the future, it put my mind at ease just knowing I had one. After all, I think making the decision to make a plan is one of the single best plans any of us can ever make. Indecisiveness and the inability to problem solve eats away at us (or at least me) one day at a time.

This is exactly what was happening to me, until I said those words. Before they were spoken, I spent every single day wondering how I would get through the next hour, day, and year—not only because I no longer had tennis, but because I no longer had a purpose. That day in 2013 when I made that commitment to myself, I didn't have it all figured out, there were still five years to go—but I had a plan.

The days, months and years without tennis continued to pass, and they never got easier. I once had a conversation with someone who genuinely thought that the longer I spent beside the court and not on it, the easier it would become—that I must have just gotten "used" to it, and that I had become immune to the inability to play.

The truth was the complete opposite. Remember that I didn't begin using a wheelchair until 2017. So with each passing day that I was unable to play for the next five years, I was also unable to do all those once simple tasks. I couldn't go for a walk, carry Landon or even a glass of water, step off of a curb, stand in front of the mirror, cook dinner, clean the house, drive, work, teach Landon how to skate or play soccer, how to ride a bike, and the list goes on and on.

So it wasn't JUST about tennis. It was the crushing of everything I ever knew about myself, the loss of everything I once had been, and everything I once had. Or so I thought...

The fifth year arrived, and just like I knew I would, I stuck to my word. For those who know me well, they know that when I want something badly enough, and more importantly have decided it's what I want, there's not much that can stand in my way. It's the innate combination of persistence and determination that has been ingrained into me at my very core. I have found it to be what I need when fighting this war, and it has only grown more intense.

I immediately started researching the sport, something I had saved for this moment, because I still held out hope that this day wouldn't ever arrive, and I would run instead of roll back onto the courts. However, there I was, computer screen in front of me while I researched all the different sport wheelchairs. I found the one specifically needed for wheelchair tennis, and my jaw dropped when I also realized that it was going to cost around $7,000. I most definitely didn't have $7,000—I wasn't even working.

The idea of a GoFundMe campaign occurred to me, but I also didn't find it appropriate to start one myself—too self-serving. So, I left that idea alone, and headed to the courts with Joel, with my foldable, hospital-looking, NON proper street wheelchair.

Nonetheless, I needed to feel what it was like to swing the racquet and make contact with the ball again—a feeling I had so badly been missing for five long years. We finished an entire basket of balls and headed home. Just hitting the ball was better than nothing, but it wasn't enough. I wanted to play, and I couldn't do it in a foldable hospital chair.

Feeling slightly deflated, I knew I would find answers, I just had to keep searching. Not too long after, good tennis friends of mine discovered an old tennis wheelchair which hadn't been used for a while, and was being stored at a different tennis club. Amazingly, they rounded it up, received clearance for me to borrow it, and delivered it to me at the Grimsby Tennis Club. I was overwhelmed with gratitude, and I hadn't been so excited for anything other than Landon's arrival in the past five years.

Although an older model, the same necessary fundamentals of the sport chair were present, with the most important being the cambered wheels and anti-tipper on the back, to allow for quick turns and to prevent ME from tipping over. I didn't care how old it was or what It looked like. I couldn't get strapped into the chair fast enough, and once I embraced the first feeling of independence while navigating the court—it was an immediate flood of emotions.

I felt a surreal sensation of invigoration, empowerment, pride, and independence. Five long years, and here I was, across the net from friends I used to play with regularly. It was emotional for all of us—it still is as I write this now—and I think it always will be. It was a pivotal moment in my journey of self-reflection and self-transformation.

Just as quickly as I got on the court, I also realized how darn difficult the adapted version of the game really is. I mean, I had a bit of experience with the feeling of paralysis, but man did I experience it on a whole new level, as the ball approached me at glacial speed and I simply FROZE.

The whole idea of playing again was great, but I had forgotten I would have to figure out HOW all over again... How to hold a racquet in my hand while also trying to hold onto the chair, push towards the ball (remember the racquet still in hand), get to the ball at the right angle, not too early and not too late, and THEN remember to swing the racquet upon arrival. Piece of cake right? WRONG!

This exact feeling can be validated by my father and

many other members who have tried wheelchair tennis, just to understand what it's like— with the common response being "OH MY GOSH!" or something to that effect.

It is the single most frustrating sport I have ever tried, but I embraced it, endured it, and turned it into my single favourite version of a sport for two reasons: 1) It was my gateway to sports again, and 2) most importantly, wheelchair tennis has TRULY changed my life.

CHAPTER SIXTEEN

How Wheelchair Tennis Changed My Life

Within the same week of trying the sport, a tennis friend of ours took on the initiative of starting a GoFundMe campaign. It was shared by a multitude of friends, family and members at all the tennis clubs I had played. There are no words to accurately describe the level of generosity I experienced. Within only a couple weeks, enough money had been raised for me to purchase my very own tennis wheelchair; one that would be custom-fitted and made for me. Things got super real and I was ecstatic! I knew it would be a few months before I received my chair, since I still had to be fitted and have it made, so I continued using the borrowed chair and tried to improve as much as possible.

As mentioned earlier, I tend to move rather quickly towards things I really want, and the ability to compete in wheelchair tennis was no different. Right away I contacted OnPara, who immediately put me in contact with Tennis Canada's head coach of wheelchair tennis. He was excited I had shown such strong interest, as finding more players with this level of interest and enthusiasm is crucial to growing the sport.

I had been used to the able-bodied tournament structure in Ontario, and I thought it might be similar for wheelchair tennis, with various levels of tournaments. Well, I was WRONG on that one. The head coach told me that the only tournaments for wheelchair tennis players are at the international level, and is a professional circuit, similar to the able-bodied tour. In other words, I very quickly learned if you want to get involved with the sport at a competitive level, you have to jump right in! (Or roll right in…)

The coach then told me that there was one tournament in Ontario left on the year's calendar, and would take place a month from then. It was in Toronto, and attracts some of the best players in the world. The registration deadline had already passed, so to be accepted into the tournament, I needed to be accepted as a wildcard.

When I was asked if I would like to enter, despite the fact that I may not have all that much success, it took me less than one second to enthusiastically respond "ABSO-LUTELY!" Winning was never my concern, and I knew it wasn't even up for discussion anyways. It had been a month since my first time back on the courts, and these women had been playing for years. In fact, I was in the same draw as the world number one and several other top ten players. Meanwhile, I was still learning how to maneuver a chair that was not even mine, and ended up playing the tournament in the borrowed chair because my own had not yet arrived.

My family and I still laugh over the fact that I didn't even have a proper street chair yet, so I showed up in my oversized wheelchair-looking thing, amidst all these professional athletes, with custom made street and sport chairs. It was one of those "had to be there" moments, but was rather humorous when I was talking to the head coach in person about how excited I was to be there, and my eagerness to continue to improve and eventually participate in other international events... and he responded with something along the lines of "Wow that's great to hear Gillian! One question, are you planning on getting your own proper street chair?" Just picture "mighty ducks meets wheelchair tennis debut."

As you probably already figured out, looking good with the proper equipment, or winning on the scoreboard was low on my priority list. I was just so extremely excited and honoured to be involved in the event, to get experience with what international wheelchair tennis tournaments were all about, and to meet so many wonderful players/people who each have an inspiring story of their own.

It was surreal knowing that just one day before the tournament, I was watching these athletes play matches on YouTube at the Paralympics, World Cup, and Grand Slams... and then there I was, introducing myself to them and learning about their story.

That was the tournament and moment I officially became a competitive athlete once again. I found out there was another tournament in Vancouver in a couple months, and it didn't take me long before I found myself registered, and on the courts at least once and sometimes twice a day with either my dad or Joel, trying to improve. I worked as hard as humanly possible with MS in tow, and in just two months, my dad and I were on a flight to Vancouver!

Since then, I have played in twelve international and three national wheelchair tennis events. I continue to strive for improvement every time I am on the court, and although there have been recent changes to my life (which I will expand on later), wheelchair tennis still remains a crucial part of my life and well-being. It has been the absolute best thing to happen to me in recent years, and the best way to showcase all the ability I still have left. After spending the last two and a half years competing in events, playing against some of the best players in the world and watching them play against each other, I don't even see the wheelchair most of the time. I just see incredible people and outstanding athletes.

For once since my diagnosis, it was no longer about what I CAN'T do and rather about what I still CAN. Since this moment of enlightenment, a snowball reaction began, and I started gaining back multiple aspects of myself, which I had recently lost.

How Wheelchair Tennis Changed My Life

REGAINED INDEPENDENCE

It all started the moment I stopped resisting a wheelchair, and got my mobility back. With regained mobility, I succeeded in my persistent pursuit to be an athlete again. Next, I spent days researching an appropriate vehicle, which had enough space for a lift to be installed, but would not be a "mom van." Nothing against all those who are rocking the mom van, but it just wasn't for me.

Once I found my vehicle (Honda CRV), I spent the next week or so researching any grants available for the lift/hand controls, but soon figured out that a tax credit was the best and quickest option to get me back on the road. It was winter 2018 and it had been a year since my doctor was obligated to take my license away. I totally understood this decision, but it was still a massive hit to my independence. If you are ever wondering what a loss of independence feels like, start relying on everyone else to take you to every single place you need to go.

It may not feel so bad at first, especially if you are still able to walk and do everything else for yourself, but over time it is suffocating. Luckily I had family willing and able to help me, but it is still one of the most restrictive feelings, other than the paralysis I feel every day. SO, it became very obvious to me, that in order to further my quest to regain my independence, I needed my license back. After all, that new Honda of mine wasn't going to drive itself.

I had to start from the beginning with the computerized test, which I thankfully passed without studying for—and then took the required lessons I needed to take with hand controls. After just twice behind the wheel, my instructor from APEX driving, felt I was ready for the road test. Meanwhile, I had no other way to practice for the test, because I didn't yet have a vehicle with hand controls installed, nor a license. I am happy APEX felt confident in my abilities, because truthfully I was still trying to figure out if it was "push" or "pull" for the gas.

Fast forward a week and test day had arrived. I was nervous as heck, just like the first time when I was only a wee teenager. Wow, how time flies! I concentrated almost solely on not confusing the brake with the gas, remembered to check my blind spots like a relentless parrot, and made sure I didn't crash into anything. IT WORKED! A big celebration was in order—after almost two years without it, my license was again valid. I still had to wait ten long days before my new vehicle was equipped with the lift and hand controls, but it was well worth the wait.

Similar to the first time back on the court, it was an empowering, freeing and invigorating feeling. So why stop there? Winter 2018, and so far I had gotten back my mobility, the sport I love the most, and my ability to drive. Regained independence on fire! But there was one major piece missing...

Ever since my last day of work in 2014, I envisioned what it would feel like if or when I'd work again. I became more regretful each day for having taken the ability to work for granted, and thought how lucky others were who could still work.

As the days, weeks, and months kept ticking by, and short-term disability quickly transitioned into long-term disability, each day I wasn't able to work became harder and harder. As the months turned into years, returning to work seemed so out of reach, yet I wanted it so badly—and the more days that passed since my last day of work, the more selective I became about the type of job I would return to work for. I no longer felt that I HAD to return to work, but rather that I WANTED to return to work, and only for the "right" position. I had ideas about what this perfect position would entail, but could never put my finger on exactly what it would be.

So I remained patient, determined and hopeful that I would one day find a position I loved, for a business I believe in, and in an industry I couldn't be more passionate about.. and FINALLY after four long years, I found all of those things at Niagara Academy of Tennis.

September 4th 2018 marked my first official day as the Sales and Marketing Director for Niagara Academy of Tennis, and the first day in four years that I could say I was no longer on disability. Although I had already been approved for long-term disability to age sixty-five, that's not how that part of my story would end. I demanded more from myself, and I wasn't willing to give up or to give in to some illness that didn't deserve any part of me in the first place.

And once again, just as it felt to regain the sport I love, independence through the use of a wheelchair and the ability to drive, my first day re-entering the workforce felt the exact same way: SURREAL, EMOTIONAL, and EMPOWERING.

SO, to sum up this massively important part of my story, I've learned that the only disability capable of preventing us from reaching our full potential is our own self-doubt, absence of want, and lack of determination. For anyone reading this, who for whatever reason is now confined to a wheelchair—Please, NEVER think life is over. NEVER EVER for a single second think you can't do the things you once did, such as competing in sports, working, driving, and being mobile—because you absolutely, positively CAN. It is a matter of finding other ways of doing these things.

If I have proven nothing else in this entire chapter, I hope I have proven this: a wheelchair isn't disabling at all. For those of us who are no longer ambulatory, it is a tool in our "life kit," which enables us to do all the things we once thought we'd never do again.

It may not be our favourite accessory, but once we learn to embrace all the regained independence it provides, the next thing on the list is regained confidence. Once this state is reached, you likely won't even see the chair nearly as much as you once did. I can say with 100% certainty, that there are now days when I don't see the chair at all. Allow it to be an empowering tool for you, rather than a hindrance and life as you see it will be forever changed.

Against all odds, you CAN do it.

CHAPTER SEVENTEEN

Braver Than Your Battle

Blog Excerpt:
"The Little Engine that Thought it Couldn't"
February 11, 2018

I hear you- strong and courageous one...

I hear you chug chug CHUGGING along at the very back of the bunch. I can feel your effort, your exhaustion and your pain. I can feel your teeth gritting together as you take one small yet ever so important step after the next. I can feel your hands sweating as they grip ever so tightly onto whatever it is you are relying to keep you up right.

My hands shake along with yours as you try to propel yourself forward just one last inch. I can feel your anger, your frustration, your disappointment, your fear, and most importantly your determination.

I know it's harder for you than the rest. I know you look ahead and wonder why that can't be you? Or maybe even more accurately, why that's NOT you anymore?

I know it has been a long time since you have felt the

effortlessness of lifting your legs, something similar to the feeling of floating in a salt water pool.

I totally understand how defeated you feel when the rug beneath your feet feels like fur, and I know how scary it is NOT to know what the next thing is you will trip over.

I can resonate with you ever so deeply when you say that you just don't know what "normal" feels like anymore, and that you simply can't even IMAGINE what life must be like without pain.

I place no judgement whatsoever on the days you break down in tears, have the ugliest of ugliest cries, or scream at the top of your lungs and surprise yourself at how off pitch you can be.

I don't wonder for a single second why you are more sensitive on some days than others, or why you feel a LEGIT celebration is in order for solely cooking your own meal.

I understand to the nth degree why you feel like throwing yourself your own damn fiesta JUST for cleaning your own room, and why HECK YES, walking to the end of your modest 1,200 square foot home, DOES deserve a champagne popping party EVERY. SINGLE. TIME.

I know YOU know, that you have 50,000 reasons to scream, while also realizing you have 50,000 more reasons to smile. I also know, it just doesn't always feel as such.

I know you are grateful for SO many things, while at the same time wondering "What the FAAAAARRRIG" is going on in my body?

I know you are happy for others going through great times in their life, yet also feel empathy for those who are going through struggles of their own. I know you're a good friend, a good parent, a good child and an overall great person.

But if nothing else, I want you to know that I get it. I get how you feel and I know you are trying. I know you are trying to be strong, to be grateful, and to be kind. I know you are trying your best to simply keep trying and I know you are ALWAYS trying your best to keep smiling.

I also know it's not easy. I know it's not easy to sometimes feel like a burden on others, yet continue to surprise those same people with the many triumphs you endure.

I know it's not easy to get dressed in the morning let-alone dressed up, and I know on SO many days it would be so much easier to just NOT...

To simply NOT get up, to NOT get dressed, to NOT smile, to NOT be kind, and to NOT be grateful.

Yet you ARE.

You may be the slowest, and most worn out one of the pack, but you are also the mightiest, bravest, most courageous and most experienced, because this reality is YOURS. It's yours in every single essence it embodies, and YOU my friend, have become the veteran of it all.

It will NEVER become easy, but in so many ways you have mastered the art of making it appear so. You will ALWAYS cross that finish line no matter how disadvantaged you start OR with how many huffs and puffs you exude, because after all, YOU are the little engine that COULD and YOU my brave warrior are KILLING it!

CHAPTER EIGHTEEN

Life Happens

It's interesting this thing called life. When we are younger, in our toddler and adolescent years, we don't have a care in the world. Our sole responsibility is to be a child, live freely and fully, and to our highest potential. We don't fully understand the consequences of our actions, and that's okay, because we are learning. We are constantly evolving and always discovering how to do something new. Eating, crawling, walking, running, talking… Every single day we are learning something new. We start school, learn routine, develop friendships, and learn that not everything always goes our way.

As we become teenagers, we get bored of the way we once lived, and envision a perfect world with no rules, no one to tell us what to do, no homework, no heartbreaks and no responsibilities. Most of all, we often develop an inaccurate "I know everything" mindset. Our parents can suddenly do no right, and we can do no wrong. We think life is tough when our best friend betrays us, or a boy decides he likes someone else. Failing a test in Geography can seem like the end of the world, and being excluded from a party can be absolutely heart wrenching—and at that stage of life, those feelings can feel completely accurate.

Remember: the only version of awful we know is the one we are experiencing or have experienced before. Perception is reality. We are built from experiences at every stage of life, and we therefore cannot be expected to know how bad it can really get, when we have never experienced anything worse than a battle over a toy at two years old, or being the victim of the class bully at age sixteen.

We enter into early adulthood, and watch ex-friends, ex-boyfriends, new friends and familiar faces navigate through this new phase of life. Engagement, marriage, first home, kids, and sometimes a less celebratory milestone— separation and eventual divorce. No one goes into any phase of life predicting the failure of that phase. No one gets pregnant, predicting the terrible misfortune of a miscarriage. No one gets engaged expecting to be left at the altar—and no one gets married, expecting it to end in divorce.

The above is completely accurate in my journey—my story. Joel and I had many great times in our marriage. We built a life together, including the birth of our beautiful son Landon. Although it was far from perfect, from the outside looking in, it appeared flawless. The qualities I admired in Joel in the beginning, are still qualities I admire about him now, and ones that make him a great father. His unmistakable work ethic, determination, kindness, and generosity will always be a part of his character.

We had a nearly eight-year-long marriage, and although there were fundamental differences in our personalities, there were also similarities. Tennis was obviously the commonality we originally found, and spent a lot of time at the courts, until I was no longer able to play. The five years when I was unable to play were trying times, and although we eventually got back on the court through wheelchair tennis, a level of damage had already been done to our relationship.

For the last two years of our marriage, we struggled more and more to find common ground surrounding various issues, and unfortunately, we were faced with adversity that many couples will never face.

As mentioned, Joel knew about my MS since our third date, and he was supportive of me and what we may face together. But that being said, neither one of us could predict that within a year, I would face mobility struggles, and would be immobile within two years. Joel stuck by my side, and I will be very clear when I say that the reason for our separation was never because of Joel "giving up" on me. He stuck by my side and helped me complete everyday tasks. He took the burden off of me both physically and financially.

Over time, as I was still resistant to a wheelchair and couldn't access the laundry room downstairs, more and more household chores fell onto him. Although he was there for me through it all to the very end, it would be misleading to say that MS didn't take a toll on our marriage. Rather than spending time as husband and wife, it is my belief (and quite possibly his too), that difficulties arose when our relationship turned into patient/caregiver. I don't think we totally realized it at the time, but we have had recent discussions about this (post separation) and we both agree that this played a major role in the breakdown of our romantic relationship.

After many discussions regarding the future of our relationship and attempts to rekindle what we once had, we decided to part ways in November 2019. I initiated this, and although we have a friendly co-parent relationship now, we went through a very difficult phase, as most couples going through a separation do. We both said things that were out of rage, out of character, and unnecessary. Luckily, this phase didn't last too long, and as expected, everything got much better between us when I moved into my own place, giving us true separation.

Since this book is about my journey, I feel it is important to be completely transparent about another specific detail. Near the end of our marriage, I met someone at a work conference in Vancouver. We had an immediate connection, and although this was not the reason for the connection, it turns out he also has MS. It therefore became very difficult for me to pour 100% back into my marriage, when my heart was partly elsewhere and I no longer had 100% to give.

Near the end of our marriage, I was not honest with Joel. During this time, he was trying to do some of the things I had asked of him many months and years ago, but I had already mentally "checked out" of the relationship (for lack of better terms), and therefore was not very receptive to these gestures.

Although we knew that the most difficult aspect of our separation would be the effects on Landon, we also knew that remaining together would create an unhealthy environment for him.

Even though we considered ourselves separated in November, I remained at the family home until I had a different place to move into. I started looking right away, as I knew there was not much on the market, especially in Grimsby and within my budget. Staying in Grimsby was my first choice to be close to Landon as well as my parents, and we had already agreed that I would have him for six days out of fourteen and every other weekend. Pick-ups and drop-offs would simply be easier if I lived in Grimsby; close to Landon, Joel, and my parents who also lived in Grimsby and continue to play a huge role in Landon's life.

It was difficult to predict where I would end up living, as when I first started looking, there was nothing in my budget in Grimsby, and the only reasonably close location was Stoney Creek, Ontario. It wouldn't have been the most horrible option, but certainly not the best. I lost hope that I would find a place in Grimsby, until a two-year-old condo came up for sale, and my real estate agent and I, along with my dad, checked it out immediately.

The same evening, I decided to make an offer, and immediately found out there was also another offer going in, forcing me to decide if I wanted to be in a multiple offer situation. The condo had only been on the market for less than a week, and obviously was popular. Fully renovated, and move-in ready, I could not give up on it. I decided to go in with a strong offer and hope for the best.

The next day, I had just arrived at my hair appointment, when I received a text from my real estate agent: "We did it! Congratulations!" It was a bittersweet feeling. I was excited that the place was mine and that I would be able to stay in Grimsby, but it didn't call for a celebratory champagne toast, as it had with the first place Joel and I had bought together. This was for a very different reason. Instead of a step towards a life together, this was a step away—and although I wasn't second-guessing the decision to separate, it still represented a ten-year chapter of my life coming to an end, and was time to start a new one. A new chapter which would require my independence to progress, and one in which I knew I would learn even more about myself and my ever-annoying condition.

That being said, I knew I could do it, and I knew I would be okay. I had already decided this in my mind, and regardless of the difficulty I would face, I constantly replayed in my mind many sayings I continue to live by: "you only know how strong you are, until being strong is the only choice you have," OR "I am not what happened to me, I am what I have chosen to become," OR, "You either get bitter or you get better, the choice will always remain yours." SO, it was my choice to make, regarding how I would react to my new reality.

The memories will always be there, as they were when I was packing up my things in the old house, and unpacking them in my new condo... The birthday cards, anniversary cards, and Mother's Day cards written on Landon's behalf. I knew the love was there, and reading earlier cards, it became obvious that the nature of it had changed since the first couple years of our marriage.

Both Joel and I agree that we will always hold love for each other, for the people we are and the parents we are to Landon. However, we both wonder if we were ever truly "in love" with each other. When it really comes down to it, I truly feel that we were either never truly compatible, or became incompatible due to circumstances we faced. We didn't have the type of communication needed, and over the course of our relationship, although we made attempts, we never truly spoke each other's "Love Language" (*The Five Love Languages*, Gary Chapman 1992).

That being said, I have told Joel how much he still means to me as a person, and as a father. I have apologized for my part in the demise of our marriage, and especially apologized for my disloyalty in the last six months. I know I hurt him, and my actions caused him to second-guess everything we ever had. I definitely understand, and always wanted to just tell him, but ironically enough, I was worried about hurting him. He knows I am sorry, and he has apologized for his part and the hurt he caused me at various stages.

Even though I was the one to initiate the separation, it was extremely difficult as I knew how much my family and everyone else love Joel. I knew all the great qualities in him, but my heart could just not get to the place it needed to be. I knew announcing the separation to my parents and family would not be a popular discussion or decision—but we only have one life—and just as much as I knew I would not be happy in the marriage, I also knew it was not fair to Joel. He deserves to be with someone that is deeply in love with him. Everyone deserves that, and we just couldn't be that for each other.

I knew my parents would also be very worried for Landon and the reality that I would be living on my own, forcing me to gain even more independence than I already had in the past couple years. As expected, they weren't happy with the decision, but I know it always has come from a place of love. Once some details were further explained to them, I knew it would just take time for wounds to heal and for everyone to get to a mutual place of betterment and understanding.

I also knew that the worry of me living on my own with a chronic illness and in a wheelchair, would always be in their thoughts, but I also knew that with more time spent in my place, and the more settled I would become, the further my independence would develop. I would be able to prove to myself and others, that I would be just fine—and in fact more than simply 'fine.'

When something needs to be done, no matter how fatiguing or how much pain it may cause, I have and will always find a way. I have come to master the art of distinguishing between a need and a want, and realizing I only have so much energy in the bank, and therefore priorities need to be made.

Wherever I go, I always have a plan, because if I can kill two birds with one stone I will. This usually involves minimizing the amount of transfers I need to make in and out of the car (the biggest challenge being transferring the wheelchair). The best example I can think of is hitting up strip malls where I can buy multiple things I need and MAYBE just MAYBE get my nails done while at it.

I'm always thinking four to five steps ahead, to ensure I can tick off as many boxes as possible with one trip—and I REALLY have to have an internal debate over how badly I need any one item at the grocery store. Is it worth it? Is it worth the fatigue? These are the types of discussions I constantly have with myself, and ones that are necessary to keep a manageable level of functionality to my life.

The point is, I'm doing it. I know my life is different from others, maybe more difficult, but also easier than MANY others. "There's always someone who would love to have your bad days..." There it is again, constantly on repeat. When I say no quote has ever resonated with me so deeply, I mean it.

Regardless of what my life is—harder, easier, or similar—it makes no difference to my approach to living it. It will always be a combined approach of effort, strength, determination, confidence, humility, gratitude, and a flame that continuously burns from within...never allowing it to burn out and always allowing it to burn brighter or deeper whenever necessary.

Even though my parents wished the separation had not happened for understandable reasons, they have gotten to a much better place of acceptance, and show me unconditional love and support every day. Landon too, has gotten into a routine of having "three houses" as he puts it—mommy's, daddy's, and Grandma's/ Nonno's. He is excited to go to any house, and he even mentioned to Joel and I that it makes him very happy we don't argue anymore. We both have forgiven each other and are at a much better position to co-parent in a positive manner.

Being a mother has been one of the most difficult yet rewarding aspects of my life. Children aren't born out of choice. They didn't sign themselves up to be caught in the crossfire of a divorce, and it is therefore our responsibility and obligation to keep that from happening. Sure, as parents we make mistakes. As human beings, we are fallible, and being perfect one hundred percent of the time is impossible. It is also impossible to say that we can and will try our very hardest every single day.

There are and will be days when we as parents lack the energy (whether mental or physical) to give 100% effort, and that is okay. It is okay to have "off" days, but what's not okay, especially as a parent, is EVER giving up—EVER deciding to not find a way to improve your child's atmosphere.

Joel and I know we weren't and aren't perfect parents, and we also came to the realization that we are better parents living apart than we were together. We know Landon deserves to feel happy because we don't bicker anymore, and we are all thankful that THAT phase of our separation only lasted a short time.

Although we're no longer married or living under the

same roof, we will continue to better ourselves and respect each other, so that we are in the best position to provide Landon with the "better" side of ourselves as much as humanly possible. Joel and I may not have agreed on many things throughout our marriage, but the one thing we do agree on, is that Landon is the absolute BEST thing to have ever happened to us.

BRAVER THAN YOUR BATTLE
Blog Excerpt:
"From Your Mommy with MS,"
May 2nd 2019

Dear my sweet baby boy,

From the moment you were only a figment of my imagination, I knew things would be different for you.

After your daddy and I got married, it became a long debate whether we would have you or not, one of over two years actually.

I knew for the longest time, since I was barely an adult myself, that one day I wanted a child just as perfect as you.

For your mommy, it was a non-negotiable, but there was a barrier placed in front of us, making the biggest decision of our lives also the most challenging.

We went back and forth between wanting you so badly, to then wondering if we were being fair to you. We didn't know how much my condition would have a negative impact on your life, and if there was one thing we knew for sure, it was that we wanted you to have the most fabulous life possible.

I wanted you to grow up having access to all the things I had in my childhood... Involvement in sports, a loving family, and parents who could be active with you until past the point of your own adulthood.

We knew without a doubt that we could nail the first two things on that list. We knew you would be loved beyond measure by us, your grandparents, aunts, uncles, and countless friends, and we knew we would be able to expose you to soccer, tennis, and almost any other activity that spiked that little interest of yours.

However, the last thing on that list was one we were only half confident about...

We knew that unless something unforeseen happened, your daddy would be the star of the "active parent" show, and mommy would merely be cheering from the sidelines. This my love, was why the decision to give you life was filled with so much hesitation.

I knew how badly I wanted to be the co-star with daddy. I wanted to be the very BEST mommy you deserved and I wanted to be able to do everything that most other mommies could do.

I wanted to be able to hold you while I walked and twirl you in the air while I listened to your ever-sweet giggles.

I wanted to be able to take you for walks as many times as you enjoyed, and I wanted to be able to nurse you, as that's what I heard would be the best for you.

I wanted to be the one who could take care of you more often than not, and I didn't like the thought of not being the first one you looked for when you needed something.

It was scary knowing I would have to ask for so much help, and that I wouldn't be able to get to you before every little stumble, or to halt a gummy bear going directly into your mouth after hitting the floor.

It was upsetting knowing I wouldn't be the "super-mom" I once thought I'd be.

It was very difficult knowing I wouldn't be able to make you every bottle, feed you in the night, conquer all your stinky diapers, or wipe away all your tears...

It was absolutely heart-wrenching to know I wouldn't be the one to teach you how to skate, how to swim, how to kick a ball, or to simply play chase with you and daddy in our beautiful backyard.

I knew how many things I would miss out on doing with you and for you, and I was absolutely certain there would NEVER be a day I wouldn't wish I could do more.

BUT the thing is my dear, these were all thoughts I had before I actually became a mommy... YOUR mommy that is...

All the wondering and hesitation finally came to a point when we realized that no matter the hurdles or obstacles thrown our way, and despite knowing how difficult it would be, we knew we just HAD to have you. We knew you belonged with us.

All those prior thoughts were ones I had BEFORE I got to see your adorable little face and feel your itty bitty body for the very first time.

They were thoughts I had before I found out for REAL how truly amazing you are, and were thoughts I had before knowing how much you would change my perspective of "Mommy-hood."

On January 2nd 2015 at 4:43 am, after 2.5 years of indecision, nine months of complete mayhem and eighteen hours of NATURAL labour, YOU Landon Fernando Cruz, changed my entire world.

The moment they laid you on my chest and I heard your powerful cries for the first time, there were no more thoughts about what COULD be and instead only thoughts of bliss, love and disbelief that you were finally here.

It was no longer about what could possibly happen, it was about what WAS happening and our new reality evolving.

All the moments I imagined being difficult were just that...DIFFICULT...but you made it so much easier. In just the first year of your life, you showed signs of empathy, intuitiveness, and compassion. You were seriously the BEST baby EVER.

Instead of fighting the endless list of things I couldn't do for you, I learned to embrace the help offered. Your Grandma and Nonno have been by our side not only throughout my pregnancy, but every day since you were born, helping mommy so that you could feel all the love you deserve in this world.

Instead of being jealous I wasn't your main go-to person, I became extremely grateful that there was always someone to go to. Whether it was your daddy, Grandma, Nonno, Zia, Zio, Tia, Auntie, Uncle, or one of our friends, I found comfort knowing you would always have a hand to hold, and multiple people to guide and protect you throughout this unpredictable life.

Instead of wishing I would be able to nurse you through every feeding, I began to see your "Superdad" evolve, up in the night for every feeding, so that your mommy could sleep uninterrupted. I began to realize that nursing WOULDN'T be the best for you for two different reasons:

1) Mommy had to go back on medication and 2) Bottle

feeding allowed so many people to help me with this task, and through this, you were able to bond with your entire family. Since this time, you really never hesitated being held by anyone, and to this day, you are still the life of the party!

I began to learn that it didn't need to be about what every other mother could do...it needed to be about what we could do together, and what we could do as a family. You made me realize that it was okay to NOT be the "Supermom" I always wanted to be.

You showed me that the most important things I could do for you were to simply hold you, nurture you, kiss you, and love you. You taught me in your own adorable ways that Daddy, Grandma and Nonno could tackle so many tasks mommy was unable to do, and they did them with joy.

On top of loving you to pieces, I became very thankful for their ability to take you for walks, feed you, change you, and play with you, and I know they will always continue loving every second they spend with you. I remain very grateful for the special place they have in your life, as if it were not for them, your life would not be as blissful as it is.

Through knowing that you are so well taken care of, I realized that I too, play a pretty crucial role in your life, as I will always be your mommy. Coming to this realization made everything make sense, and made everything I couldn't do so much easier.

As you rapidly grew out of your baby years and into your four-year-old self, you continued to make it so easy to be your mommy, and I want to thank you for that. I know that due to my MS, you have been forced to grow up a lot quicker than most children your age, and have been exposed to a world which many will never see.

Thank you for understanding when I can't get you something right when you ask. Thank you for being patient with me when I can't do things as fast as others can, and thank you for all the days you have compromised to play catch rather than soccer.

Thank you for becoming the most compassionate little man I could have ever hoped for, and rubbing my legs when you know the pain is too much to bear.

Thank you for candidly explaining to random people why your mommy is in a wheelchair, and not having a care in the world regarding the stares you may not even notice you receive.

Thank you for your unbelievable attentiveness, using your "tools" to fix my wheelchair, and for all the hills you have pushed me up.

Thank you for recognizing my challenges and loving me nonetheless.

You are more than just my SUN, MOON and STARS Landon... You are my constant reminder that a "Supermom" doesn't come in one single form.

In the mere four years of your life, you have witnessed more than some will in their entire lifetime. You have helped to bring me out of depression and instantly created a fulfilling purpose in my life.

You have taught me what unconditional love is all about, and you have shown me how to appreciate the littlest things in life.

You have given me a reason to smile every single day, and have made me proud in many moments of your teeny tiny life.

It warms my heart to know how much you want me involved in almost everything you do, and it is an honour being able to call you my son.

Although there are many moments when I have to say "sorry baby, mommy just can't do that," you rarely get upset, and instead immediately suggest another way of doing things.

Are you really only FOUR? I constantly ask myself...

There is never a day I am not impressed by you, thankful for you, or in awe of you.

Despite being wise beyond your years, I know you are still too little to understand the intricacies of our daily life, or what life may look like when you are older. None of us truly know my dear, that is what makes this illness so hard to manage... We just simply DON'T know.

Nonetheless, my ultimate wish for you is that the FUTURE you will one day read this letter and understand that by teaching me to accept all the "mommy" things I'm unable to do, you have taught me how to be a "Supermom" after all.

You have taught me to be proud of my accomplishments and have taught me on the next level, what it truly means to be grateful.

As Mother's Day approaches, I want you to know just how amazing you are, and just how much you have changed my life for the better.

I want you to know that you will always be my driving force, my motivation, and my greatest love.

No matter what lies ahead for us, I want you to know that I am already SO very proud of you. WE are so very proud of you, and we will always have your back, just as you have ours.

No matter what other obstacles we are forced to overcome...I will ALWAYS be your mommy, YOUR Supermom, and your number one fan.

I know I'm far from perfect, but I love you to the moon and back.

I always have. I always will.

Love,

Your Mommy with MS

The Next Phase

Most, if not all of us have either said or been told: "As one chapter ends, another one begins." In life, it is vital that we all undergo change at various times in our lives. Whether the change is voluntary, or involuntary, it is essential to our well-being and growth that we allow, initiate, and embrace change.

But change can be scary, uncomfortable, and nerve-wracking, and many of us will try to avoid it for as long as possible. We humans are creatures of habit. We like to know where we are going, what we are doing, sit at our favourite table at a restaurant and anticipate the familiar food we are about to eat. There is a comfort in staying at the same workplace, and in the same career, EVEN when we're unhappy, because at least it is a familiar environment.

Yes, we all like to try new experiences such as a new holiday, a new food, or even meeting a new friend. However at life's very core, we are most comfortable with people we already know, places we have already been, eating foods we have already developed a liking for, being in romantic relationships in which we feel secure, and in careers in which we excel.

One of the most excruciating feelings that I experience—and I'm sure many others do too—is indecisiveness. Throughout my journey thus far, I have discovered that resistance to change and indecisiveness are very much linked and have a profound effect on each other. Furthermore, I have discovered that in order for change to influence us in a positive manner, we must be physically, mentally, and emotionally open to it. Most recently, I have found that being open-minded can also happen at a subconscious level. Often, it can be that feeling of finding something you didn't know you were looking for.

As it turns out, in my case, it wasn't SOMETHING I didn't know I was looking for, but rather SOMEONE.

APRIL 25, 2019, VANCOUVER

"Hi, my name's Sean, and I think we have a mutual friend who would like for us to meet." The very first sentence which has led me (us) down this crazy yet unbelievably exciting path of new romance.

December 2018, MIAMI

Four months before meeting Sean, it all began when I met his best friend, Mike, at an international education conference in Miami. I was attending on behalf of Niagara Academy of Tennis, and it was my first conference of its kind. I had no idea what to expect, other than long days of in-depth seminars and MANY meetings.

The conference was a few days long, and during the first evening, a welcome reception was held for all the attendees. Mike happened to be one of the seminar speakers earlier in the day, and had remembered me when we ran into each other later that evening. After several minutes of chit-chat, Mike learned about my story, and naturally learned that I was fighting the constant war against MS. He found my story inspirational—so much so, he had to call Sean right away and tell him all the details.

The phone call likely wouldn't have been so urgent if Sean didn't also have MS. According to Mike, Sean knew of others with Multiple Sclerosis, but none who had a positive outlook on the illness or their "new" life. Two years before I met Mike, I wouldn't have fit the mold of positivity either. As explained throughout this book, it took a lot of time for me to get to the place I was at when I met Mike. Two years earlier, without A LOT of self-development, I would have been just like all the other negative people Sean had already encountered.

Mike didn't say much else about Sean, and in fact he didn't even tell me his name. Until we met in person, four months later, I only knew of him as the "best friend." Time ticked on by, and when I was told I would be attending the conference in Vancouver, I looked forward to catching up with people I had already met, like Mike, but the thought of meeting Sean never entered my mind. It probably had to do with the fact that I hadn't heard anything more about him since that evening in Miami.

On the second day of the Vancouver conference, a colleague and I decided to head to the hotel bar for a couple drinks. I ran into a few agents I knew, as well as some other delegates I had met in Miami. I was expecting it to be a relatively early evening, but it turned out to be the complete opposite.

According to Sean, the evening went something like this: He was standing at the bar with two other delegates who were also close friends of his, and it wasn't too long before he saw me rolling into the bar with my colleague. He didn't know with certainty that I was "the Gillian" whom

Mike had told him about, yet he felt compelled to abruptly interrupt the conversation he was having and said "sorry, but I have to go right now and buy that woman a glass of wine."

Without further ado, he did just that, climbing over three other people to get to me, while politely excusing himself, and extended his arm to greet me. "Hi, my name's Sean, and I think we have a mutual friend who would like for us to meet."

As soon as I acknowledged that I did indeed know his best friend Mike, he knew that I was in fact "the Gillian" he had heard about four months ago. The connection was immediate, and it was intense. Although MS was our common thread, and should have taken up the majority of our conversation, it didn't.

Soon, all the other agents around me had left, as did the rest of the patrons, and it was only the two of us left in deep conversation. The depth of our connection was pure and it felt like I had known Sean for years. There was a level of comfort which I will never be able to accurately describe.

However, I was still married to Joel, and Sean was still in a relationship of fifteen years, which was on the brink of its demise. At that point, neither of us thought that we would form an unfathomable romantic relationship, and just simply knew that in some form, we would always have each other in our lives.

Time passed, and the more Sean and I talked, whether over the phone or through text, our connection intensified. Without much effort at all, our connection blossomed, and this was one of the first indications that we had something rare. But we continued to have this strange "push and pull" aspect to our bond, as we both were committed to other people, and knew the feelings developing were more than just a friendship.

I saw Sean in July at a wheelchair tennis tournament in Vancouver, and a few other times when he came to Ontario for work conferences. Despite our initial resistance and attempts at distancing ourselves, it was not in the cards. We knew it would be a long road ahead, with pretty much everyone against our decision, but our future together became more and more inevitable.

All the questions we knew others would ask, as well as ones we asked ourselves were constant, with one weighing the heaviest: "How would we make this work?" Living 4,100 kilometers apart, with him having a son and daughter, and me with a son of my own. We never could come up with any practical answer to overcoming this hurdle—yet still, we knew we could not say goodbye to each other. It got to the point where we tried envisioning our lives without each other, and then it hit: there was no suitable or acceptable way to NOT be each other's romantic partner. This was the realization that led to one of the most substantial life changes for us both.

I knew that the development of my feelings for Sean, meant being dishonest in my relationship with Joel. I have told Joel that if there was one thing I could go back and change, it would be to tell him about Sean, instead of hiding it out of fear of hurting him. I know now, that by trying NOT to hurt him, I did exactly that. It is much easier now to say that I would have just told him, but when in the moment, many emotions were running rampant.

As mentioned in an earlier chapter, Joel and I struggled with our marriage for a couple of years before our eventual separation. We had many talks about being happy, even if it wasn't with each other. So, although Sean was a catalyst in getting to this decision, he is not the reason for the breakdown of our marriage.

I am not at all proud that I was unable to be honest when I should have been, and there are no ifs, ands or buts about that.

After the official marriage separation in November, Sean and I discovered more and more about each other, and although initially an unpopular decision to those around us, our relationship became exclusive.

The truth behind the façade of any single person's life is almost always well-disguised and something we will never fully uncover, unless provided with explicit details, not readily available on social media.

At the root of every decision a person makes, is a reason. A reason that may seem right or wrong to an observer, but regardless, there is a reason. It is not our job to find this reason, but rather to focus on our own reasons for progression, change, or betterment of our own lives.

Close family and friends may or may not be invited in, but the best thing we can do as a close support, is listen. This will likely lead to uncovering pertinent details, which may change our entire opinion of what we once thought was so black or white.

I have come to believe that more often than not, people initiate change in their lives in pursuit of happiness, or the betterment of themselves. Sometimes it is hard to believe someone isn't as happy as they appear, due to all of the forced smiles and posed shots on social media. Joel and I would often hear we were a "power couple", when really we weren't. Things were never horrible. But being just 'okay' is far from fantastic, which led to the change I knew I needed to make in my life.

Having the prognosis of your future altered in less than sixty seconds, really validates the statement "life is too short." We are on this planet for such a short period of time, and we owe it to ourselves to make the changes necessary, for us to be far more than just 'okay.'

Often, being okay doesn't really mean okay—it means the longing for something deeper—something that ignites passion you don't even realize you have. Sean did this for me. He was and is someone whom I am not willing to let go. We have ignited a new found passion in each other.

Regardless of the potential thoughts such as "wow that is way too soon," or "OMG she met him when she was still married," or "how selfish is she?" I am still following the path I want, feel is best, and the one I know I deserve. The lesson to be learned, is that it doesn't really matter how soon or how late, or how right or how wrong—there will always be opinions, and there will always be AT LEAST one person who won't agree with how you choose to pursue your own happiness. However, the salient question should always be "Do YOU agree?"

Only you know the whole truth and the key details. We are not always proud of every choice we make, but there are two important choices I have made regarding my future, within a single year: 1) to end my marriage, and 2) to develop my relationship with Sean; decisions I made independent of each other. When I ask myself "Do I agree?" with these decisions, the answer to both is YES every time. Regardless of all the opinions others have or had, when I take the time to run an internal self-assessment, I am a happier person now than I have ever been.

I have come to understand that the best choice isn't

always the easiest or most popular choice. As a human being, you will NEVER please everyone, and this isn't your job. However, it IS your job to figure out what makes you the best version of you, despite the adversity you face, and then do THAT. Do whatever THAT is—whatever makes you happy and sets your soul on fire. When you reach the point of self-fulfillment, you will naturally become the best mother and partner... the best YOU—the "you" you're proud of. At least that's what happened with me.

CHAPTER NINETEEN

Mine

As I have navigated through the last decade of my life, I have had moments of vulnerability, strength, empowerment, determination, and pride—but I have also had moments which I would describe as nothing other than the most horrific, weak, trying, and traumatic times in my life thus far.

I have been dealt cards I didn't want, and I made no effort to understand them, nor entertain the thought of them becoming my new reality. I have lost more than I ever fathomed possible, and I drowned myself in self-pity. I have screamed and cried at every failed treatment, and every drug that didn't take the edge off of the horrific nerve pain I've been forced to face EVERY. SINGLE. DAY.

I spent many days taking microscopic steps, and dreaded each time I had to get up for any reason whatsoever. Remaining upright meant grabbing onto anything sturdier than myself for balance. I felt no purpose in life, and spent many days wondering why I was even here.

I spent sleepless nights causing near paralysis during pregnancy, and wanted to slap anyone who mentioned having a simple cold. I had no patience for those who felt sorry for themselves without having a "real" problem.

I became a pro at the fake façade—the fake smile, pose, and caption. Making people believe I had it all under control… that I just had to fight; fight it every day and I would be okay. That despite the chaos and utter disaster my life had become, I would be okay…

However, in reality, I nearly broke at every single moment that I appeared to be "okay" but wasn't—losing the ability to walk, work, and drive, and never having the ability to be the mother I always thought I'd be.

I went through those long trials: CCSVI treatment in Mexico, PONs Device in Montreal, Mesenchymal Stem Cells in Ottawa. All of these equalling HOPE. The reason for doing any of those, or any treatments in the future will always be hope. Hope that one day I will walk again, live pain-free, without worrying about the future, or the mother I need to be.

I was resentful, angry, and far from the person you would want to be around. "WHY ME?" on replay, never getting an answer. I thought about the worst possible prognosis, and wondered how long I would get to be a part of this wonderful yet confusing world.

I isolated myself and was unable to attend major functions such as weddings, baby showers, birthdays, and funerals, due to one ONCE simple task… WALKING. I did all the things someone with no hope for the future would do… I couldn't feel gratitude. I missed my old life so deeply and so desperately. I wanted it back so badly.

I wanted to run, skate, skip, and wear heels again. I missed me, and I didn't know what to do. I didn't know how to go on and create a beautiful and meaningful life for myself. I pondered this every single day.

I missed tennis immensely and the competition of athletics in general. I tried to be supportive of others who were still able to play, and despite the inspiration I may have brought to them, I hurt—not being able to do what I had once been able to do hurt SO deeply—and the eventual decision was made, that it was no longer beneficial for me to be a part of the tennis club in any capacity.

I went through every single negative emotion possible. I had given up on any type of positive future. My life was ruined and now it was mine to deal with. I was exhausted from the moment I opened my eyes and just so DONE with medical appointments. I didn't want to wait in another examination room, waiting for hours to go through all the riveting parts of the neurological exam, and in the long-run—that therapy wasn't "the one" anyways. SO many attempts ending up not working. I was sick of it, sick of it all. The illness, the pain, the prognosis and every discussion about it. I was DONE.

But here's the thing: there are times in life when we CAN'T just be done. It doesn't work that way. We don't have the right to give up when we feel we can't go on—not for our sons or daughters, mothers or fathers, partners, and certainly not for ourselves. We have to somehow manage, deal, hold on and press on, find the strength we never knew we had, and find ways to discover a new normal- Other ways I didn't know existed, but I could not and would not remain in that depressed and deflated state for the rest of my life.

And it was around this time of hitting an emotional rock bottom, when I stumbled across the quote that changed my entire perspective of life and my journey on this earth: *"There will always be someone who would love to have your bad days."*

I talked about the "split-second" that changed my life in the first chapter, and here I am in the last chapter, thinking about an entirely different split-second. This time a positive split-second. The split-second that occurred immediately after resonating with that quote.

It all became so true and so clear. At the end of the day, my battle is my battle, often turned into war—but there are others fighting battles of their own (some far worse) at all points of life. Instead of focusing on what I had lost, I started focusing on everything I still had. I started practicing gratitude and let go of what I could not change. I fought harder than ever before, and made it my mission to NOT fall victim to my illness, to NOT isolate and make horrible decisions about my future, to be stronger than I've ever been before, and become bigger and better than this illness. To rise above despite all the reasons to not...

I grieved the loss of myself, and transitioned into a new self, with a new perspective. I regained the ability to drive using hand-controls, and I regained the ability to work, despite having a free pass to be on government disability until age sixty-five. THAT was never a viable option for me... I knew I still had so much to offer to this world, I just needed to discover it all.

Ever since my newfound perspective, it has been under development, with layer upon layer being discovered. I stopped feeling sorry for myself, and started looking for opportunities to inspire others. I started a YouTube channel and a blog (braverthanyourbattle.com), and engaged in some public speaking events.

I knew there were so many others struggling—whether with MS or without, they were struggling. My approach has never been to limit my message to "MSers" only. I want anyone facing adversity to be able to hear or read my story, and relate to any part of it, if at all.

When I was at an emotional rock bottom, someone's wise words brought me out of it, and into a place of appreciation—I want to do the same for others. I hope others facing rock bottom can read even a part of this book, and find motivation and the deepest determination to be braver than their battle.

When I decided to get my life back, I stopped focusing so much on what I had lost, and created the best possible plan of action to be independent. It was obvious that the inner confidence needed in life, stems from independence. While I reflected on this, I noticed that a new confidence can be built, just like a new normal—wheelchair or not, I knew I could be confident again, and that is what I focused on building.

I am more confident today than I have ever been before. I am far more grateful and appreciative. I know now that waking up is a gift, not a right, and despite the storm that may await, it is my personal duty to become the very best version of myself... To become the best version of myself right NOW, not in some far-off future.

And as I started to navigate this new world of zest, gratitude and determination, I had one powerful thought, and I knew if I ever wrote a book, I'd feel compelled to share it—something crucial and vital to becoming anything other than what we currently are.

PURPOSEFUL CHANGE

Becoming a happier person doesn't just happen. It's not just something we stumble upon for no reason. Overcoming adversity doesn't just happen. We don't just get stronger without experiencing the trying times. The new versions of ourselves, don't just create themselves due to chance. The decision to lead a purposeful life, despite tragedy, isn't made by someone else on our behalf.

We all lead our own personal journeys, with our own personal struggles and tragedies. We all have our own moments of desperation and triumphs. But it's up to us to decide what we do with all that—all that life throws our way. "We can either get bitter, or we can get better—the choice will always be ours."

CHOICE is what everything comes down to and where everything collides—go left or go right. Push forward or pull back. It's a game of chess, of decisive moves, and sometimes we don't make very good ones. But when there is a move, there was a decision, and it was initiated by YOU.

It is YOU who decides to see the better side of life despite a tragedy, and play the heck out of the cards you're dealt.

It should therefore never be about the journey we feel we should have had, or the one for which we were "destined." It should never be about the journey led, controlled, or influenced by others. It should never be one that suits another, or in spite of someone else.

Our most positive, passionate and purposeful journey is the journey we make. The one we embrace despite our circumstances. Whether walking or wheeling, the only life we will ever get is the one we're living.

Through the reflection of all the heart wrenching and heartwarming moments, the triumphs and trying times, and the adversity faced and overcome thus far, I realized to the very depth of my core that being 'The Girl in the Wheelchair' is REALLY not that bad.

ABOUT THE AUTHOR

GILLIAN MAURO is a Grimsby Ontario native, born in 1987. At only the age of twenty three she was delivered a debilitating diagnosis which has changed her entire world and has forced her to live life in a wheelchair. Gillian is a Brock University grad with a degree in Sport Management and has a wealth of expe-  rience in the sales industry. In addition, she has a passion for writing and engaging in motivational speaking events. She is a dedicated mother to her five-year-old boy Landon and has regained her ability to be a competitive athlete after overcoming much adversity.

During her darkest days thus far, someone's wise words helped to shape her new found perspective on life and it is now her goal to inspire others through the release of her very own book. Gillian wants those facing battles of their own to find inspiration through the details of her journey, so that they too can believe in the greatness in life despite their own adversity. Gillian also has her own blog (braverthanyourbattle.com) and invites anyone with questions or comments to reach out to her through this platform.

Made in the USA
Coppell, TX
31 July 2020

32089441R10079